South of the Northeast Kingdom

DAVID MAMET

South of the Northeast Kingdom

NATIONAL GEOGRAPHIC DIRECTIONS

NATIONAL GEOGRAPHIC
Washington D.C.

Published by the National Geographic Society
1145 17th Street, N.W., Washington, D.C. 20036-4688

Text and photographs copyright © 2002 David Mamet
Map copyright © 2002 National Geographic Society

Library of Congress Cataloging-in-Publication Data

Mamet, David.
    South of the Northeast Kingdom / David Mamet.
        p. cm. – (National Geographic directions)
    ISBN 0-7922-6960-8 (hc.)
        1. Vermont–Description and travel. 2. Vermont–Social life and customs–20th century. 3.Vermont–Social life and customs–21st century. I. Title. II. Series.

F55 .M34 2002
974.3–dc21
                                                    2002075116

One of the world's largest nonprofit scientific and educational organizations, the National Geographic Society was founded in 1888 "for the increase and diffusion of geographic knowledge." Fulfilling this mission, the Society educates and inspires millions every day through its magazines, books, television programs, videos, maps and atlases, research grants, the National Geographic Bee, teacher workshops, and innovative classroom materials. The Society is supported through membership dues, charitable gifts, and income from the sale of its educational products. This support is vital to National Geographic's mission to increase global understanding and promote conservation of our planet through exploration, research, and education. For more information, please call 1-800-NGS LINE (647-5463), write to the Society at the above address, or visit the Society's Web site at www.national-geographic.com.

Book design by Michael Ian Kaye and Tuan Ching, Ogilvy & Mather, Brand Integration Group

Printed in the U.S.A.

To Howard Norman

CONTENTS

South of the Northeast Kingdom

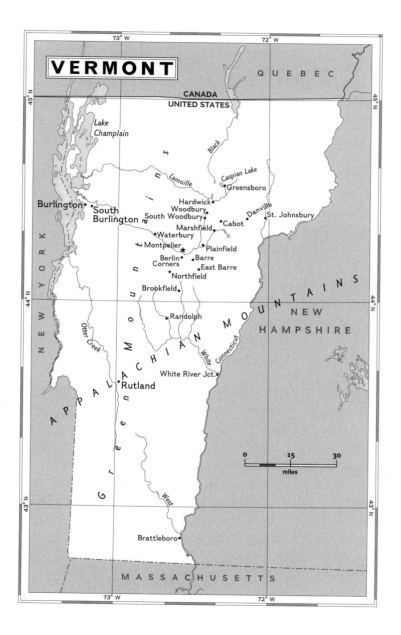

Vermont

The catamount ran across the road. What was that?

The mind slipped a bit at the sight of a lion in the wild.

There is an education in the sight of a bear—wherever did one see that black before? Not like a bear in the zoo, not like a domestic animal—not, indeed, like anything one had seen before, but wild like the call of the wolves, like the barking of the deer torn down by dogs, like the communion of tracking an animal, the ineffable sense that, as you are thinking of it, it is thinking of you.

There are those human senses that we all acknowledge, but which we cannot quantify. The girl at the stoplight turns as she feels your gaze. No conscious effort can bring about this result; it is a survival of a primal, an occult, powerful part of life.

Similarly, there is a mystery in the evanescent. It surfaces,

certainly, at birth and death, but it is present regularly, intermittently, just beyond, and different from a conscious knowledge.

I felt it in Vermont.

CHAPTER ONE

The School Year

September, this is when the year begins. So say we Jews, and so say we theatricals and schoolchildren.

The year begins when it turns cold. This is the start of intellectual activity.

The day, as in the Bible, begins at dusk—it begins not with birth, in the spring, but with conception. In the autumn. The leaves fall from the trees, expelled by the first beginnings of the new bud. That is when the year begins.

Just as the day begins with rest, with reflection, with knitting up, as the Bard said, of the sinews for the new thing.

The day, the season, life, begins with a dream, in quiet and cold.

Fall is the season in which I heard the ghosts. In Vermont, in Newport, in North Hero, in East Montpelier.

In Newport, in September, at the home of the Civil War

impresario, in the 1970s. The landlord was his aged daughter, then in her nineties. She showed me, in the barn, the old house board advertising one of her father's triumphs: *Julius Caesar,* starring Junius Brutus Booth, Edwin Booth, and John Wilkes Booth, the only time the family troupe appeared together. A painted house board.

Thirty years later, in my barn in Vermont, there is my own house board, William H. Macy, and friends, in a play I wrote and staged as a youngster—in transition toward the antique.

The house board is in the woodshop, covered in the sawdust of the wooden animals I've made for my children. So false, so artificial; that is not the kind of man I am. I am a *city* man. But, thirty years later, there they are, seventy or eighty wooden animals, scattered around the shelves, in boxes, in various homes.

The first was a farmer. Ten inches high, red shirt, blue jeans, a leather-billed denim cap (which, just this last summer, went missing). I painted him in thick, uncut oils—took ten years to dry.

We have the moose, a slab of wooden antlers correctly athwart his head. We see the other moose down on the pond, frequently. Down the hill from the house.

We see them first thing in the morning, last thing at night. We look out the kitchen window to see if our moose are there, to see if the bear is back. We've seen the bear on the pond twice—once a sow with a cub.

Quite startlingly beautiful, as black as anything you ever saw.

Around the house we have hawks, bald eagles, owls, foxes, coyotes, wolves—the animals I carved and put on the shelf.

A tradition that began as artificial, and so could be continued only through force of will.

Much like the habit of measuring the kids against the cabin walls. Those twenty years of marks.

Edwin Booth made a speech to the nation after his brother killed President Lincoln. I often read the speech. It was framed and hung in his house on 20th Street in New York. The house became the Players Club and I was, for a while, a member. He wrote in apology to the American public, asking it to believe in his horror and his shame, and shock, and in his wish for an early grave.

The story of John Wilkes Booth never rang quite true to me. It took time for the missing piece to emerge, which it did, perhaps, like some foreign fragment in a wound, working itself to the surface.

For it was too pat that the assassin was an actor, that the murder took place in a theater, the shout of triumph from the stage.

It became clear to me that Booth was trying not to kill the President, but a congruent potentate: his brother. For Edwin Booth was the premier actor of his age, and John Wilkes was no one, the forgotten younger son.

His ambition and rage were projected upon the President, who died for an actor's envy; and John Wilkes Booth, quite literally, became the most famous figure ever to tread the stage.

Old graveyards.

Rudyard Kipling lived in and loved Vermont. He wrote in *Two Seasons:*

"Hot summer dies, behold, your end is near, for when men's need is sorest, then come I." An admirable conflation of birth and death that, not to let the cat out of the bag, is the essence of Vermont.

What greater perception of peace than the depth of the woods at twenty below, when the power of rest, the beautiful completion of death, infuses one with an overwhelming sense of order.

CHAPTER TWO

State and Nation

The mind of a writer, like that of a child, functions most happily in independent discovery. The child's precious, joyful, idiosyncratic investigation of the world is such an essential part of its nature that it can be eradicated only by education.

I have contracted to write a book about Vermont, and so find myself obsessed with Indiana.

I have just discovered Edward Eggleston, an exceptional Hoosier writer of the end of the nineteenth century.

His book *The Graysons* is a murder mystery. A fellow is wrongly accused, and in peril of forfeiting his life to the state. He is saved only by the efforts of an unknown young lawyer, Abraham Lincoln.

Eggleston writes in his preface that the events, though surprising, were related to him independently by several of the figures of the drama, who actually knew Lincoln.

I count the book a discovery—in addition to being a delight—as the story of *The Graysons* is the story of John Ford's film *Young Mr. Lincoln,* the best of the Lincoln biographies.

Lincoln's excellence at the trial, portrayed in the film by Henry Fonda, is, then, a part of the country's mythos—but it is such only as it has been twice fictionalized, last by screenwriter Lamar Trotti, first by Eggleston, based on earlier reports. It is true to (and thus included in) the myth because it *rings* true. (Like Parson Weem's story of George Washington and the cherry tree.)

Eggleston's story is also part of the place-myth of Indiana, which, in the early nineteenth century, was the West. He pictures it, in its settlement, as the best of anarchism: a locus of independent, pioneering, but withal fair-minded folk, who could band together for this or that communal requirement but understood their destinies as under their control.

The current debate over "The Star-Spangled Banner" ("rousing, historic, but unsingable") nominates "America the Beautiful" as a possible successor. Opponents suggest that the song, while a nice enough tune, praises the pastoral; that, as such, it is merely nostalgic, indeed elegiac, for an America we urbanites do not know.

But I must disagree. How much of our national character derives from geography? I am a Jew, born in Chicago in 1947. My race and generation were raised to be leery of the notion of the Homeland. We identified the concept with Nazi Germany and *Lebensraum.*

We revered and revere the veterans of World War II—my father's war. We understood the propaganda of that war as

WILLIAM H. MACY

iconography, intended to express rather than to foment national sentiment. We knew our parents to be patriotic in a matter-of-fact way—that they fought and suffered for America not because it was the Land of the Free, but because they lived here. They had as little connection, really, to Fort McHenry—or, for that matter, to Appomattox—as my children have to Normandy.

I worked with a man who'd been an Army Ranger on D-Day. He landed "first wave, second boat" on Omaha Beach.

I introduced my fifteen-year-old daughter to him, and searched for the words to help her understand with whom she was shaking hands.

The gap, at the time, was unbridgeable; and would she in later years study history, the memory will be forgotten. It was a moment not for her, but for myself; an attempt to make sense of history, of nationality.

The obscenities of the postwar period, the McCarthy witch hunts, the Vietnam War, turned many of my generation against the notion of nationhood—the Hollywood Ten, the Vietnam vets had been betrayed by the duplicitous and self-seeking, who wrapped themselves in the flag.

How did the Nazi *Lebensraum* differ from the Monroe Doctrine, we ask, or the Nisei internment from the Bataan Death March, or that from the Trail of Tears?

The answer, of course, is that we live in a political association, that human beings have the capacity for evil, and that conglomeration tends to foster it—abstracting individual human actions from individual consequences.

The political process is a sad conundrum. In the name of history, reason, and loyalty, we debase and are debased.

Our politicians seem to be the hirelings of raptors, of the large corporations that fund their campaigns. Perhaps there are exceptions, and certainly this is the way of the world, but one must sigh.

For just as a village reputation is seldom wrong, a national consensus is hardly ever right. How can it be? Our country is too vast, we are increasingly hurried, and our information, in the main, is sold to us—at stultifying cost—by the same organizations that buy and sell our elected officials. Well, decay is the way of the world, and one may read Spengler or the Tower of Babel and find the same tale: "My name is Ozymandias, king of kings; look on my works, ye mighty, and despair."

Saki wrote "Happy the land without geography."

Vide: America—swollen from sea to shining sea, its current proprietors the wards of two rather large oceans, and content to ascribe our hegemony not to Neptune, but to some indistinct and ineluctable excellence. What is national character? Canadians are placid, Americans are brash, and the border is an imaginary line. We must, therefore, adduce at least an admixture of tradition and education as part of a national character, if such exists. Regional character, we know, exists. There is a Southern gentility, a southern California vapidity, an upstate New York gloom.

How can one be uninfluenced by geography? One cannot. We all are affected at the least by the weather, which is specific to geography. And this is a beautiful country, so perhaps geography can inculcate civic pride, and thus perhaps civic virtue.

I loved to stand on 57th Street in New York, around sunset, around Seventh Avenue. At that height one could look to the east, look to the west, and see to the two rivers in that thrilling late-afternoon light.

It felt like love to me. As it did in Chicago, near the lake, even in that cold which freezes the inside of the nose, and gives you that copper, blood smell, which seems to live in the back of the head; or in Los Angeles, at night, which is the only time the city comes alive.

It is a beautiful country, and we are all fortunate to live here. Not because of the snow at Valley Forge, and not because it was hallowed by our fathers—such can come dangerously close to an arrogance, say, an assertion of excellence, which is the unfortunate side of patriotism. We are fortunate to live in a place with ample food and water and generally controllable or delimited depredations both by industry and politics, where

officials of public safety, justice, and security of commerce are, in the main, accountable to the citizenry—to live our lives, in short, in the Four Freedoms.

I was in a small plane, flying from Toronto to Boston, when New York was bombed. In the ready room at the small airport where we landed were pilots, businesspeople, and mechanics, grouped around the television replaying the towers' destruction. On their faces one saw sorrow. This was not the jingoism of "Tell it to the Marines" or the obscenity of "peace with honor," not the shameful trickery of "The liberation of Kuwait has begun" or "America—love it or leave it."

This was not the fool rhetoric of "feeling another's pain," which is only a sick entertainment, but grief; and it doesn't exist without love.

This was not the America of bombast and self-congratulation, but sorrow for the good that we recognize and participate in as the fellow feeling of those who share a simple blessing.

I've always felt that love and commonality in Vermont.

CHAPTER THREE

Post-and-Beam

American flags blossom on homes and cars after the World Trade Center attack. The Jews daubed blood on their doorposts to avert the Angel of Death, and we display the flags similarly.

They are, of course, an expression of solidarity, but there is that of the apotropaic about them—deliver us from evil.

Two months after the attack, anxiety, in our small community in Vermont, seems higher, somehow, than in the cities. Perhaps, up here, we are just closer to our neighbors. We rely on one another more. A drought, a severe snow, a power outage—for that matter, a divorce—affects us all. This commonality of feeling might be called a shared or mutually recognizable humility.

American schools argue about requiring the Pledge of Allegiance—in Vermont there is a real recognition that we

live under God; or, differently, that much of our lives is beyond our control.

The Vermonters, like the Scots and the Irish from whom they descend, are necessarily philosophic. It is not a parlor game, but the practicable wisdom of living in a harsh world.

The Scots have a reputation for being close. They aren't close, they're just smart. Like the Vermonters.

One must be smart to hunt successfully. The deer are smart. The quiescent, slaughter-tropic cartoon creature is a down-country fiction. The successful hunter does not boast his triumph over nature, rather he acknowledges his acceptance of its laws, and endeavors to better understand them.

My best afternoon hunting was a lazy afternoon on a ground stand.

I was still-hunting through the woods, and heard a far-off

shot. I knew the big deer liked to bed in a blowdown up that way, and now they would be moving. The prevailing wind was northwest, and I put the shot beyond, that is, upwind of the blowdown. The deer could not move in its preferred upwind pattern, as that was debarred by the hunter. It could not move east, as the brook lay there, with its steep banks, and the deer, moving downwind, would be loath to expose itself on the banks. No, the deer must move south, and indeed southeast, to put as much distance as possible between itself and the hunter.

So I took a seat, and faced north, and in a while here came the deer, left-to-right, as if I had willed it to appear. My delight and astonishment cost me the shot (it is called "buck fever"), but I would not let a technical failure erase the pleasure of an instance of right-thinking.

Itinerant Scots carpenters framed the ubiquitous Vermont Cape House. A team would come through, of a summer, and raise however-many homes. In their wake the owners and neighbors would clapboard the building, and there you go.

The houses are post-and-beam, hand-dug cellars, and granite-block foundations, "one-and-a-half Cape." That is, in plan, a rectangle thirty-by-forty, or thereabouts, with a low second floor, covered by a two-pitch roof.

The buildings are first-growth pumpkin pine. Post-and-beam hand-hewn with a broadax, mortised, and the joint pegged with a trunnel (a treenail), or peg, of wood, about the width of a screwdriver handle.

These houses are framed without nails, built to shift slightly in response to the seasons, and so endure.

My house is two hundred years old. When I bought it in 1978, it had been abandoned for thirty-three years, the windows broken out, snow and rain blown in. The clapboards and the window frames were rotten, but the frame was, and is, straight and true. The beams show the marks of the broadax. I consider the house a work of art. Everyone I know in Vermont lives in one. They are infinitely adjustable as they are, essentially, an empty cube. Put the door, windows, staircase wherever you want. Add on the summer kitchen, mudroom, new addition, to taste.

Some of the farmhouses stretched, addition after addition, till they reached the barn, a history of family growth and prosperity, fifty years of architecture, throwing up a line against the prevailing wind, a Vermont landmark.

CHAPTER FOUR

The Woodstove

In the winter the cookstove cooked the food, heated the water, warmed the family, dried (and burned) the wet mittens and stockings in from the snow. In the summer, out back the cookstove went. Into the summer kitchen, off the mudroom. The mudroom was and is a sort of air lock between the world and the house, the season's various distinctive and protective garments hang, drying or waiting, the wet or muddy boots litter the floor, tools, firearms, fishing gear, a butterfly net hang from the beams. In the old days herbs were dried there. Traditionally the old summer kitchen—a seasonal space—was fully enclosed as the farm grew, and became the mudroom. Then the new part was added, next in line, and gave the house the distinctive "dumbbell" configuration.

When I was young, the old cookstoves could be seen discarded alongside the road or dumped into a ravine, where one

also found the Grand Rapids oak pedestal table, each artifacts of the industrial period after the Civil War, and momentarily superseded by our friend, progress.

Today, of course, such are prized, sought, and petted as antiques. The stoves, coincidentally, continue to work quite well. For an experience of heaven, I recommend this: Bake an apple pie in a cookstove. Feed the stove apple wood and/or rock maple. Go out and smell the mingled smoke coming down in the cold.

I love these old woodstoves, their sides and front sand-cast in mythic figures, the nickel bumpers, knobs, and lifters similarly deified; relics of a different age, when the objects of everyday use were created, if not with pride, at least with reason: that the creator, the user, and so society would benefit from a concern for utility, and would in no way be injured by coincidental beauty. Or perhaps it was simply that labor and materials were cheap, and that industrial adornment was the nineteenth century's equivalent of the huckster's "Buy me!" But I do not think so.

I have a cabin out back of my house. In my cabin is an 1880s Garland parlor stove. They called it a "four hour" stove, for that was the length of time it would hold a fire.

I find this stove endlessly provocative. I've drawn it and photographed it and written of it over the years. And I have either assigned or discerned in it a personality. Its personality is not whimsy, but fact. The stove demands to be treated in different ways on different days. It reacts to changes in temperature, humidity, and, I believe, in my mood.

If I come to light the stove after any time away, if I light it hurriedly, or thoughtlessly, with inadequate consideration of the wind, or thoughtless placement of kindling—if, in effect, I take it for granted—the stove will not light. Then I will say to myself, "That's true, too," acknowledge the chastisement as reasonable and instructive, and begin again.

Rightly, courteously prepared, the stove will burst into flame with the addition of the match. Can a computer have a personality?

Inside the house is a Vermont Castings Company Resolute woodstove. These were designed and marketed as "airtight" stoves—a newfangled idea of the 1960s. The notion was that the burning gases could be superheated and burned again, or some such thing. No stove, of course, is airtight, and the wood, we all know, must combine with oxygen to burn. But the Resolute is tighter than the nineteenth-century stoves. This means it should hold a fire longer (overnight), burn hotter, and create more creosote.

Creosote is a residue of wood fire. It rises as smoke and hardens, coating the stovepipe and chimney. It is handy should you want to experience a chimney fire.

These fires are diverting. "What is that?" one says. "It sounds like an express train, or volcano, or some such"; and then, in progressed cases, the chimney starts to shake, as the creosote ignites and burns at some notably high degree. In the chimney fire *toute entière*, the house burns down.

So, especially in these days of airtight stoves, one must keep the chimney and the stovepipe clean.

One cleans the stovepipe by lugging it out into the driveway, stuffing it chock-full of newspaper, and setting the paper alight. The pipe burns hot and rather loudly, and at the end one is left with very black and loose, shalelike creosote, which is knocked out onto the ground, and the pipe replaced, leaving one with a feeling of righteousness.

I bought my Resolute in the '70s, as many of us did, and was pleased, as the years rolled by, to find the stove company provided not only an excellent product but an after-market service. They would come to the house, knock the stove apart, clean it, regasket it, reblack and reassemble it, and voilà, for a nominal charge, a new stove.

The company was in Randolph, Vermont, an hour's drive from my house. The length of the drive became significant in the case of my three daughters, all of whom were born at Gifford Hospital in Randolph.

Gifford was, and is, famous for its hospital, and for its hospital's birthing center. The midwives and doctors there treated birth as a natural phenomenon, rather than a medical emergency; they recommended and practiced natural child-birth, a bottle of champagne afterward, a knit cap for the little kid, a car seat, and off you go.

Lou DiNicola, the pediatrician, was called in the middle of the night when my first daughter was born, and he pulled on his pants over his pajamas, and came up the hill to the hospital, to see the new baby.

We all love our American icon, the country doctor. It is not that long ago that the doctor was a man *revered* by the community for his knowledge, for sacrifice, and, I think certainly, for his acceptance of this burden: He personified mythology, he was expected to perform—and generally did perform—a ceremonial task well.

Barbara Bush went to speak, during her period as First Lady, at one of the Seven Sister schools. A group there protested her presence, as she was being honored not for any personal accomplishment, so they thought, but as an adjunct of her spouse.

What a barren view. How many people have been made happier by reason than by ceremony?

Is the soldier's widow more comforted by a policy statement, or by the honor guard? All honor to the generations of physicians who sat through the night by the bed of a dying patient they had no power to cure, and to the country doctor who came by in the middle of the night to see the new baby. These acts of grace stay with us throughout our lives.

Also in Randolph we found the Brigham Gel Company, which for many decades made the theatrical gels used to light the stage and, later, the screen.

I remember these gels, working backstage as a very young

man in the theater. They were, indeed, gelatin, and could withstand the searing heat of the stage lights. Drop water on them, however, and they dissolved like the Wicked Witch.

The last scion of the Brigham clan was Bill Brigham.

I met him when he was Amtrak stationmaster at Montpelier Junction, Vermont. In those days the *Montrealer* ran from Penn Station to Montreal, and vice versa, once each day.

One worked all day in New York, got on the train at 9:20 P.M. and rode a small sleeperette through the night to Montpelier.

They woke you at 6:00 A.M. with a cup of coffee, and you pulled on your clothes, turned the bed into a couch, and watched the early morning (in winter, the night) in Vermont— improbably white smoke rising from the farmhouses, a lone pickup at the grade crossing, deer on the hillside, all the requisite, beautiful aspects of that romantic set piece.

Bill and I discovered that we had the Boy Scouts in common. He was a scoutmaster and a brother member of the Order of the Arrow, an advanced and, as I remember, semisecret association within the Scouts.

Bill was raised working in the gel factory. He told me of mixing and hand-pouring the gels into the marble drying tables. He told me of Pier Paolo Pasolini, or it may have been Luchino Visconti, or indeed Federico Fellini, traveling to Randolph to handpick gels for his film.

I would arrive at his station for the down trip early, and we would gab about the Scouts. (I had a spare leather patch from the 1960 Jamboree in Colorado Springs, and gave it to him for his collection. He responded with kindnesses those of us who

have dealt with an impersonal, indeed, computerized, travel organization may well wistfully imagine.)

How I loved to see that train pull in! They'd call from Waterbury to announce it on its way, and fifteen minutes later there it was, hooting, as it came over the trestle. Say good-bye to Bill, find the sleeperette, read a book, take a nap, and wake up in Penn Station, ready for work.

Many times on the up trip I'd walk into town over the trestle.

Two- or three-mile walk, over the trestle, up to Route Two, then east into Montpelier, the state capital.

I'd walk down Bailey Avenue to State Street. On my left was the old Coaching Inn where I'd lived for a couple of years.

State Street was the old Post Road between Boston and Montreal. The inn features a very high porte cochere, a beam overhead with a pulley to haul the passengers' trunks to the second floor. A twenty-room warren that, in the late '60s, had become an apartment building.

I was working as a teacher at that time, and remember one Christmas vacation, between paychecks and stone broke, laid up in the unheated apartment with nothing other than Glenn Gould playing Prokofiev on the turntable. Not much to eat, too cold to get out of bed—*la vie bohème.*

In those days the semis geared down at the traffic light below, on the way from a stop in town to Burlington, Montreal, Plattsburgh.

After the interstate, truck stops took the business away from the cities. Montpelier, in my youth, boasted three all-night diners, and for a while Montpelier fell on dismal times—the old businesses dried up, the farms began to disappear, and with them the farmers' demand for the big city and its services.

Montpelier got an infusion of funds for the Bicentennial, and has currently rediscovered itself as a bedroom community for the state legislature, its dependents, and the urban sprawl that is the fate of Burlington, thirty-five miles to the west.

I would walk, I say, down State Street, past the State Capitol building. It has a lovely gold dome, and is built out of native Vermont granite so clean that, at any distance, it has the unfortunate propensity to resemble cinder block.

I have had affection for the Capitol building since, in 1965, I found, in a middle-of-the-night motorcycle trip through town, a herd of deer on the lawn.

Next to the Capitol is the old Pavilion Hotel, long commandeered as a state office building.

I once had a question about my state income tax, and wandered over to the Pavilion in the hope of finding a form or instruction booklet that might put me out of my misery. I saw an office door opened, and inquired of a woman there for such a form. She asked what the problem was, and I told her, and she said, "Let's have a look at it." She did my state taxes for me. She was the state tax commissioner.

The walk also took me past the Bureau of Motor Vehicles building, across from the Capitol, where, until quite recently, they kept the driver's license records on index cards.

And in that vicinity also we find the State Law Library.

This and the country's other law libraries were, in my youth, a prized secret. I used these as a place to read, to write, and to smoke unmolested. It was the American custom, in those days, to allow smoking in law libraries. For if every American smoked, certainly every American lawyer smoked *even more*. And I smoked, too, sitting in those warm, quiet, private law libraries, reading and writing. One of the few folk in history actually to benefit from the presence of the law.

Rick Winston, entrepreneur cinéaste, had, for a while, his film series in the basement of the Pavilion Hotel. And I remember showing up one night in the early '70s to find a goat tethered to the rail outside. Picturesque, but true.

See me, then, on my cold dawn walks from the station, as I turned off Main Street, and down to the Horn of the Moon Café, just off the bridge over the river. (High-water mark, the Flood of '27: eighteen feet above street level. Still blazoned in this or that small brass plaque.)

Ginny Callan owned and ran the Horn of the Moon in best

Vermont post-hippie tradition. Good, clean food, home-baked bread, great coffee.

I'd knock on the window and get let in as they opened. Steam rose from the griddle, from the coffeepot, everyone one knew came in.

Ginny started having labor problems in the '80s.

Some of the staff thought it demeaning to work in other than a democracy, as I understand it, and began to make her life hell (the worst of the Vermont hippie tradition).

I recall the last time I went to the Horn. I settled into a table and waited for a waitress to come by. (It was understood to have become, at that point, "not done" to hail or summon a server.) So there I sat, roiling in the hypocritical foolishness of what I hope was confined to that time, for the longest time, until the waitress came by.

"I'd like pancakes," I said. She nodded and left. Another eternity passed and, as she returned, I again violated the ethos of the nonexploitive restaurant.

"Excuse me," I said. "Didn't I order pancakes?"

"Yes," she said.

"Uh, then what's the problem?" I said.

"You didn't tell me if you wanted a tall or a short stack," she said.

Sic transit gloria mundi.

Speaking of which, I see various young folk in the area attempting to relive, pay homage to, or otherwise indict the hippie period (or "Sixties") in Vermont. They seem to me infinitely dour, and have, of course, missed the point. We had fun. It was exhilarating to discover that, in fact, our parents and the Forces That Be were in the wrong about the Vietnam War, and this prompted all sorts of gnostic visions and observances. Retrospectively, how could one hope that the Revolution would not be followed by the Terror?

What a country. We follow France into Indochina, against the advice of history, self-interest, and common sense. This is the worst mistake in our American history, and we vow never to make it again. And now we follow Russia into Afghanistan. Many times it seems as if all human struggle was an attempt to apostrophize the right to blunder.

CHAPTER FIVE

Country Clothing

The savagery of civilization daily stuns me. I suppose that, pre-viously, I was just not paying attention.

Government officials are recusing themselves in droves from the investigation of Enron Corp., which fleeced tens of thousands while enriching its conspirators, its accountants, and revolving-door political proponents of "deregulation." Who are these criminals whose sense of entitlement rivals, nay surpasses that of a wasting disease? It seems to me that they consider the occasional term in office as their more open brethren in crime, the Mafia, consider a term in prison, just part of the cost of doing business.

Now I am reading the David Abercrombie Camp Outfitters Catalogue of 1938.

For a while I collected these old compendia as an aid in an abortive clothing business of mine. A couple of friends and I

started a company to manufacture American between-the-wars outdoor wear and equipment.

The inspiration came to me at a very rural diner, in a November predawn in hunting season. There were the old hunters, in their (or their fathers') rough, worn, buffalo-plaid vests, pants, jackets, in the treasured, blooded companions of years in the woods. What an affection we have for those articles that have actually supported, rescued, or comforted us—the coat that kept us warm through the blizzard, the compass or firearm that saved our life, the typewriter with which one paid the rent. I disapproved, aesthetically, of the adoption of rough outerwear as the suburban clothing equivalent of the SUV, of the admixture of irreligious man-made fibers into the cotton and wool of a more godly time, et cetera.

So I started a clothing company, and got my brains beat out, and had a lot of fun. The Joseph Morse Company, Cabot, Vermont: Mamet, Chris Kaldor, Dick Friedman, Proprietors.

I became a *garmento* as an adjunct of my love of the old catalogues. I found the old line drawings—of haversacks, folding chairs, tents, togs—dream books. For example, "Carnival Plaid: a fine warm and soft virgin wool hunting shirt. Fancy check, mixed colors, Canadian Plain combining navy blue, red, orange, and natural white, with seven mixtures of these making ten colors in beautiful harmony." What adjectives. Fine warm, soft, virgin. One, of course, wants not only to wear this shirt, but to marry it.

The colors sound like those in the woods, the shirt is made to wear in the woods, the woods are cleansing.

The rabbis said, "Put on a prayer shawl, wrap your arm in phylacteries, pick up a prayer book, *now* sin!" And, of course, the same is true of the woods: Find your water, cook your food, set up camp, build a fire, and you have little time to rob widows and orphans, or to suborn the elected.

To return: I browse through the David Abercrombie catalogue and imagine myself in the various situations for which the equipment is designed. Shall I be blamed if part of my mind creates a drama for each? And whom should that drama contain as hero?

Here we have the Silva Liquid Compass. "Fully Guaranteed against Mechanical Defects for One Year."

Ah, I say. Fully guaranteed. Those were the days.

But I have come to the catalogue fresh from the morning's paper, and so search for malfeasance.

"Why one year?" I say. Which leads me to a deeper vision of malfeasance: What risk, I wonder, does the Silva Company stand? For, should their product fail, the customer employing it cannot return to make his claim.

I find this an unsatisfactory view of the Silva Company, whose fine products I have, in fact, used since my days in the Scouts. I blame the unfortunately elected officials who have this morning debauched me. I see chicanery everywhere, and am like a man leaving a whorehouse, who now views all women as mercantile tramps.

Let me investigate my analogy. Like the man in the whorehouse, I have contracted for, and received, some low enjoyment—in my case, the gossip of the morning paper. I bought it for the gossip, and got it.

What of the beauty of chaos? The depredations of the elected must, at some remove, rival the wind through the leaves for beauty. Must they not? At a sufficient remove?

In the woods one intuits, in this chaos, a profound order—that the snow built up on this branch, rather than that; that the pitch of the wind raised or fell by such-and-such an interval. The forms of the ice on the brook, the periodicity of the thin ice, and the flowing water showing through, these must indicate, *do* indicate a profound underlying order. Its discovery is the task of the hunter, of the farmer, the scientist, and the artist. Its contemplation—irrespective of that contemplation's result—brings not peace, but enlivenment, exhilaration; and I believe our friends in Washington, blind to the fun, have, as a *pis aller*, taken to stealing the stuff of the party.

CHAPTER SIX

South of the Northeast Kingdom

My area of Vermont is circumscribed. It lies in the north of the center of the state, over to the east, and just below the Northeast Kingdom.

Draw a line between Montpelier and St. Johnsbury on the Connecticut River. Halfway down the line is Cabot, Vermont, where I have my home. I first saw Cabot in 1965 when I was a student teacher at the Cabot School. I worked there, as I remember, as part of a college course on education. I taught French, and was taxed to remember the lessons I had learned, a scant year or two before, as a student myself—thus aligning myself with generations of schoolmasters.

I commuted to Cabot on a borrowed motorcycle from my alma mater, Goddard College, some twelve miles to the west.

I attended Goddard as it was the only school offering to admit my seventeen-year-old ne'er-do-well self.

I discovered, there, an odd if energizing contempt for anything historically classifiable as education.

There, smack-dab in the midst of the turbulent '60s, we found a return to the primitive, a renunciation of literacy, and an endorsement of the time-tried indoctrinary expedients of sex and drugs.

This reversion to the gnostic was also manifest in Vermont (then and now) in a proliferation of the crafts and arts of the preindustrial period. I found, and find, in the neighborhood (a swath ten or twenty miles either side of the geographic line mentioned above) a proliferation of advanced, serious, accomplished blacksmiths, woodworkers, potters, weavers.

Here, in the mainly given-up farming communities, is an artisanal reversal, or *repeal* of the Renaissance—a dissatisfaction with the urban and industrial, and a true return to the land— not as farmers, but as practitioners of the old, home crafts.

Many writers live in the area, too. But it is by no means a "writers' community." That phrase always puzzled me, striking as false a note as a "hermits' convention." For writing, like the crafts named above, is a magnificently solitary occupation. One works by oneself all day, longing, wondering, dreaming, supposing. All attitudes to which Vermont conduces.

When I was a lad in Chicago I frequented the bookstores. Volume after volume said, at the end of the writer's bio, "He lives in Vermont." So I went to Vermont. To pretend to go to college. And stayed on, as it is beautiful, and as it is the perfect place for a writer to live.

It is various, remote, interesting, challenging.

My friend Anita said that one can be many things in Vermont, but it is hard to be lonely. I have found this to be true, as, obviously, have these other craftspeople.

And perhaps the profound order of the environment seduces, as much as does the solitude, to contemplation.

There is, to skirt the mystic for a moment, something in the land. It is different from New Hampshire, which I have always found a dour place, its geography reflected in its inhabitants. There is a spirit in the countryside itself. Some places have it, some do not. San Francisco is exhilarating; one cannot say the same for Detroit.

So Vermont has garnered (and, of course, formed) several generations of new (post-World War II) artisans, those practicing the farm skills without the farm—a group, to tax the conceit, closer to hunter-gatherers, perhaps, than to the agrarians.

Perhaps we are like settled nomads. The skills are, arguably, the nomad, the portable skills—and the talents of the writer merely the formal contemplations attendant upon practice of those skills, absent the hard artifact. What forms the scale on the fire-hot iron, why does the twist in the wool reverse, how will the tenon expand in the heat? This interest in the minute, in the seemingly chaotic, is also the concern of the writer.

I played the piano as a child, and pitied the poor fools lugging the bass or the tuba to their music lessons. What better than to travel light?

Writing requires a pencil and some paper.

In Vermont the children and I have cut goose quills into pens, made ink from soot, and written on birch bark. It is a game, but there is a seriousness in it. It is one more thing one could do cut off from industry. It is one less category of things to crave.

Seneca cautions that we should always treat fortune as if she were going to do to us everything she has in her power to do. And this consciousness is part of the Vermont mentality. It is a part we interlopers admire enormously. One could hunt for food. If the ammunition was gone, one could hunt with a bow. There is water in the stream, and water in the 1800s hand-dug well; one can heat with wood.

These considerations and their partial practice have a large place in the fantasy of the urban writer, down home on Le Petit Trianon. But their practice is salutary, even in very small doses. They challenge one, in the old phrase: Make it last, make it do, do without. Or as IBM had it: Think.

CHAPTER SEVEN

Skill and Education

The Sloyd knife was, until the 1950s, a tool familiar to every American boy. The knife was a fairly straightforward one-blade affair, with a simple, hand-filling wood grip, used for rough carving, trimming, or filling.

All American boys, I think, loved shop.

Almost all the true teachers of my youth—those worthy of attention—taught the physical: sports, music, shop.

The heartful term of respect, to us, was not "teacher" but "coach." He was the fellow who could do something you wanted to do, whose job it was to teach you, to make the difficult easy, and so enjoyable; in short, the perfect model of a teacher.

The title was not infrequently tinged with love, as he stood *in loco parentis,* if not in extent of authority, at least in esteem.

Who would not want a physically adept, patient parent?

Philosophical attainment might not be evident to a child or to an adolescent mind, but physical prowess coupled with respect for the neophyte, these made a powerful impression.

In our pantheon the shop teacher was, of course, Vulcan, the Lord of Iron, which, Mr. Kipling reminds us, is "master of them All."

He was overseen, in the (to the young mind) idiot adult hierarchy, by the principal, a distant Zeus, and by the assistant principal, one of the Furies—our first view of frustrated ambition expressing itself as rage.

The various teachers we understood as placeholders, to whom we students constituted that drudgery to which they, in turn, subjected us. (The child mind, I believe, understanding it a regrettable but at least comprehensible operation of "Turnabout is fair play.")

Those grouping themselves under the banner "education" by that act announced their renunciation of desire for any human contact. But the music teacher, gym teacher (occasionally), shop teacher, coach, these we understood as human beings.

The guidance counselor I seem to remember being viewed as a spy—a pathetic attempt at dissimulation on the part of the administration. Viz., "Behold, we have nothing to hide. We put before you one of our functionaries, part of the table of organization of our own bureaucracy. How could you mistrust the motives of one who will not hide his reviled antecedents?" (A sort of Wernher von Braun, if you will).

I remember such counselors as paragons of good fellowship, moderating and pleased to be seen moderating their revulsion at my dismal scholastic performance in a determined effort to help me make something of myself.

The actual *folk,* the shop teachers et al.—they had nothing to hide, and so nothing about which to lie. They were not protecting their dignity—who doubted it, when they were engaged in the practice of demonstrable and desirable skills? They did not, therefore, revert to authoritarianism. Yet their classes were a good model of discipline.

Discipline—that fear-word of my youth. "Those who do not succeed lack discipline. Those who lack discipline cannot succeed. They are weak, and will go through life a failure."

In retrospect, perhaps the more "disciplined" of my colleagues merely lacked the emotional makeup to be depressed or confused by the meaningless, the sham, and the arbitrary.

I did love shop. I turned a maple bowl in shop. I learned to type in typing class, a skill I employ every day. I learned the rudiments of cooking and the operation of a sewing machine.

Perhaps if teachers, if elders want respect, they might do something that merits it—perhaps teach the children a skill.

Educators complain that they are hidebound by the strictures of school boards, who complain that they are in thrall to the budget, to the laws, to publishers.

Those in charge subject the children to constant meaningless testing, whose rules, scoring, and operation invite (if they are not, indeed, designed to require) complicity and fraud.

"What can I do?" the educators whine. In this no doubt legitimate complaint, the young see their elders infantilized, and passing the burden of hypocrisy and drudgery down to their charges. "But what can I do?" they complain, and wonder why the students don't respect them.

The Sloyd knife. A Scandinavian word meaning "skill," as in *sleight* of hand.

A child is impressed by patience, strength, humor, and skill. Schools, rather than inculcating these virtues, seem to exist to devalue or destroy their admiration. The farm life, of course, required skill for mere survival.

Farming, hunting, fishing—the professions and pastimes of Vermont—were either practice or abstractions of the most basic human endeavors: agriculture, hunting-gathering, war. They formed the mind to respect the wisdom of nature: The unobservant farmer will starve. They taught the body to prosecute the dictates of the mind, and they hardened the will.

Ethan Allen said, "I am as determined to preserve the unity of Vermont as to preserve that of the Union; and before I saw it sundered, I and my hearty Green Mountain Boys would take to our Beloved Hills, and make war on all Mankind."

All machines are limited. The more elaborate the mechanism, the narrower its application (there are myriad things one can accomplish with an ax, but only one thing with a photocopier).

Superelaborated organizations (the computer and the corporation, for example) work, in fact, to effectively and progressively narrow their possible applications. The Red Cross, post-September 11th, withheld monies that it had solicited for distribution to the victims. "The organization" decided that its ongoing purpose and needs would be

better served by this unilateral decision than by a knee-jerk adherence to its word.

And a computer cannot spell "kerf."

The machines are images of ourselves—easygoing, perhaps, indeed, lazy. We trust our machines, and then, in mindless acceptance, come to endow their operations with a magic sanctity, ceasing to compare their utility with their original advertised purpose.

And so we accept not only their obvious limitations, but their increasing imposition and inutility—having invested in their rectitude, it is simpler for us to accept than to constantly override their imprecisions. Eventually—with the computer, as with the electoral college, or party politics—it is cheaper to *endorse* the inefficient (indeed, the absurd) than to doubt what appears as the "given."

We accept that "the Government" is not to be trusted, and hope to find that it will, occasionally, contain this or that human being who might, through chance or whimsy, act in our personal interest. We vote for these folks on what we are told is their "character," wagering our national fortune, our environment, our foreign policy on the backs of those persons least caught-out having illicit sex. The computer's spellchecker, designed as a tool of communication, teaches its operator not to use the word "kerf."

Steve Bronstein, the blacksmith, instructs me to bend my knees when I bring the hammer down. A traditional martial arts technique, an ancient technique.

"Let the hammer do the work," he says. The usual image of

a blacksmith is wrong, he says, one doesn't need the massive arms. All of the blow is in the wrist, let the hammer do the work, and bend the knees.

Kate Smith, the weaver, works on an old wooden loom for a living. Her leisure hours are spent in even more basic weaving; she shows me the warp-weighted loom, in effect, yarn hung from a beam, the bottom of the strands tied to rocks.

Charlotte the potter, similarly, forsakes the fine work on the wheel to show me ever more basic pottery technique, the pot hand-formed of coils of clay.

Eric, the master chairmaker, designs and forges his own tools at a small portable forge. Originally he used store-bought woodworking tools, but found them unsuitable to his anachronistic work practices. He sought out and copied nineteenth-century woodworking tools and found that they, too, didn't quite answer. The grain of modern woods, he told me, differs from that for which the originals were designed. So he became a designer and blacksmith in order to make a chair.

Modern, statistical life rewards the ability to choose the approved among four alternative answers. True intelligence, on the other hand—that intelligence which approaches wisdom—consists of the ability to formulate the question.

Afternoons, I'd write. If I'd written a passage I thought good, or if I was particularly frustrated, or in fact had any possible excuse, I'd stop and sleep on the cabin couch. In the winter I'd wake in the dark, and walk back to the house, often breasting the deep snow that had fallen while I slept.

I recall the year or two the red fox lived at the top of the rise between the cabin and the house, and the year or two the rough-legged hawk lived there. I recall the sound, more than once, of a barking deer being torn down by coyotes in the woods, and the insane wail of the coyotes or the wolves at night. It sounds like pure evil.

I recall the northern lights, and other strange lights in the sky on more than one occasion, and the Milky Way and the August meteor shower, in the deep black nights, and the Big Dipper and, in opposition, Cassiopeia rotating around the pole.

New Year's night of the millennium, we were out on the pond. We'd shoveled off a skating rink, and ringed it with small brown paper bags filled with enough sand to support a lighted candle. Up near the bank, we built a vast bonfire.

On those cold nights I felt as if I wanted to give up, to be drawn into the woods, into the void, and good riddance to all the human folly and personal folly, and my own shortcomings, and despicable illusions and ambitions, and just let it go. Captain Marryatt wrote: "It is a bad World, and I thank God that I have lived in the woods."

Similarly, in the snowstorm, in the woods, skiing, or hunting, when everything except oneself was clean, and one thought how lovely it must be to die.

The land informed and informs everything I've done since I've lived here.

One so wants to hold on to it—old-fashioned New England. Now, in this latter time, it is difficult not to become apocalyptic.

So much devolves into eschatology, and one wonders if Y2K was an accurate prediction—an ancient understanding of periodicity—or if a Western civilization, sensitive to that prediction, is merely working to actualize it. Or if the two are one.

The climate changes. One reads, certainly as long ago as the eighteenth century, that it was commonplace for one to say, "The winters were colder when I was young."

Human perfidy, though, seems constant, generally free of the constraint of either shame or fear. Do I exclude myself from this jeremiad? I do not. But, at least, while I was writing I was not sinning. "Put on a prayer shawl, phylacteries, pick up a prayer book, *now* sin." Structure the same gag around a rural life, and at least in my fantasy, witness the same beneficent effect. I see the romantic residue of Vermont humor, self-regard, circumspection, and patience; call it culture or philosophy, it is quite the most attractive thing.

Proverbs is an astounding compendium. It might do well as an airport book of how-to and common sense. Tolstoy, likewise, reminds us that only shallow minds speak of "in these times"; that human nature is always the same.

"The stone which the builders rejected has become the cornerstone."

I built a stone wall. It marks a short leg of my property, perhaps three hundred feet, and undulates at between two and a half and three and a half feet in height. Vermont is dotted with these walls. The farmers lugged the stones out of the fields and used them to mark boundaries, and they are endlessly pleasing. One comes across them in the given-up woods, brush the snow off and have a seat, or sit leaning against them for their heat in the summer.

What a beautiful history of endeavor and thought—see how they capped this piece, see how it complements that.

To lay a wall and have it standing after two hundred years is quite a feat. My wall is falling, here and there, after twenty. I did love building it. Here is an odd-shaped stone. Turn it this way or that, it will not square, set it aside, and now and then, by magic, its asymmetry completes an otherwise unbridgeable gap. Perhaps all of us artists like to think of ourselves that way. Of course we do, the *lusus naturae* who fit nowhere particularly, and then not for long.

As A. J. Liebling said about boxer Billy Graham, "He's as good a fighter as he can be without being a hell of a fighter." That's what I think about Robert Frost.

But perhaps he was ruined by his subject matter—as, most probably, am I in this book. Perhaps this part of New England (he was from across the river) is too beautiful, too complete, to write of other than reverentially. The changing of leaves in Vermont is one of the few events or places in life it is impossible to overbill. However much one hears them praised, however much one hears or employs the adjective "indescribable," it will surpass any first viewer's possible expectation—it will delight, like Jerusalem, like Venice, like any first true love: shocking, were it not so incontrovertibly benign.

I remember Burlington in the 1960s, a dying lake town, once the queen of inland navigation, now in decay. I remember driving out on the ice, half a mile out, the sky was so black, and the stars, et cetera.... Burlington, of course, is now famed for its sea monster, an oft-viewed if apocryphal ichthyosaur of some stripe, who makes him- or herself intermittently perceivable to the worthy. We are told that Lake Champlain bears this or that resemblance to Loch Ness, and therefore are allowed to assign to it an increased possibility of the monstrous. But perhaps the sea monster, to turn momentarily Jungian, is merely the messenger of the unconscious—a prehistoric survival rising to our notice from the depths of our savage inner mind, to remind us of an idea more basic than civilization.

For the Burlington Malto plant is gone, that purveyor of maple-flavored breakfast cereal; the lake commerce is gone, the industrial age is gone, and the Vermont farms are going. Vermont is distressed both in mind—by a superabundance of the rational and an accelerated pace of change—and in purse, by the evanition of traditional business. How timely of the sea monster, then, both to free us from the fetters of reason and to lure the wily tourist dollar. One smart critter.

··········

Is there a mystic correlation between Scotland and Vermont?

Does Vermont differ from New Hampshire as its settlers were more predominantly Celtic than British? Eggleston wrote in 1871 that the Scots and Irish, however new to the land, throve, while the transplanted British decayed.

We read of the various attempts to conflate Scotland and Jerusalem, through the Knights Templar, the Rosicrucians, the Masons.

Does Vermont lie along some mystic lay line?

My neighbor Hugo, now in his nineties, is one of the founders and chief supporters of the American Society of Dowsers in Danville. Through the years he has told me of dowsing these lay lines, of plotting the concordance of the height, latitude, or longitude of Vermont and various pyramids, the Leaning Tower of Pisa, et cetera. He is sufficiently rich to qualify as "eccentric," and through the years I've thought that if he had as little as ten or fifteen dollars less he would be demoted to "dotty." Nonetheless.

I admire Hugo greatly. He enlisted in the Army in his late thirties, and fought through Europe with George Patton. He was a forester, he is a good neighbor, and we are friends.

Additionally, he, in his eccentricity, is merely saying things that many of us up here feel.

I have seen *damned* strange things in the woods, and in the skies.

I saw in the '60s (and again in '91) what can only be described as UFOs. They can only be described as UFOs because they *were* UFOs. Just northwest of Hugo's house.

And I have used my rudimentary understanding of dowsing to good purpose over the years. It has located the odd lost earring, and advised on matters of choice or deportment.

Q: Is dowsing not merely a concrete manifestation of a preconscious awareness?

A: Who cares? It works. The dowsers say they can find water and gold. The technique has been used for millennia. I will not gainsay it merely for its anecdoticality. I tried ratified school learning, and found it, in the main, a bunch of bunk.

Is there an inner, secret engine of the world? Of course. Indeed, several, or an infinite number.

This gnostic certainly can be perverted into evil, *vide* anti-Semitism, supply-side economics, et cetera. But however it is squelched, it can reassert itself independently, in a benign, perhaps unstated, perhaps preconscious, childlike need to believe.

CHAPTER EIGHT

A Stone Face

Cabot's Doc Caffin, rest in peace, always wanted me to join the Masons. We'd meet down at Harry's Hardware, our town's Rialto, of a morning, bum Camels off each other, and attempt to frame the existing and inevitable oddities and evils of the day in gossip, and suggest their possible amelioration.

He looked like the Old Man of the Mountains. Seventy-some years old, thin, strong, handsome, his face not deeply lined, but *riven.* I liked him enormously.

He wore, now and then, his American Legion fore-and-aft cap, decorated, as I remember, with pins denoting this or that retreat or convention, and with various pins relative to the Masons.

"Now, you know," he'd say, periodically, "no one is ever *invited* to join the Masons...."

His invitation touched me profoundly, for who was I—one of, in the words of Noel Perrin, "the year-round summer people."

Doc had served with the Navy, and was aboard the destroyer U.S.S. *Guadalcanal* when it captured the German sub *U-505*—the first enemy warship captured on the high seas since the War of 1812.

He was the Old Country Doctor, and he had gone out, if not with the horse-and-buggy, at least in the Model A days, down the back roads.

He told me he'd delivered more than 5,000 babies.

But I did not join the Masons. I saw Doc, and his wife, fifty years his nurse, at their office-home, up the Wolcott Road, his old farmhouse. He patched me up after a rather deep saw cut on my hand, and closed the bandage with Scotch tape. "Cheaper than the other stuff," he said. "Works just as well." As it did.

And I saw him at the Masons' fish fry. Moore Dam perch, caught through the ice, frozen till May. All you can eat: perch, bread, coffee in pewter pitchers, four dollars. Everybody came.

The Masons' Hall is on Main Street, across from the school—as of this writing, the last school in Vermont, K-through-12, the Cabot School. Everyone came, also, on the Fourth of July.

Cabot Fourth of July runs down Main Street, from Elm Street Bridge, just down the road from the Creamery, past the two stores, Harry's Hardware and the Cabot Village Store, past Mike's garage, past the green, the school and the church, past the Masons' Hall, and down the recreation field, the BBQ chicken, and the carnival games.

There we have the color guard. The last World War II veterans, in uniform, and carrying the M1 rifle; Larry Thompson, a warrant officer on the *Nautilus,* our first nuclear sub, in his dress whites; veterans of Korea, Vietnam, carrying the flag before their neighbors. Following them we find the fire engines, and behind them the Bread and Puppet Theatre, an internationally known group that lives in Glover, Vermont. Each year they field folks on stilts, and in papier-mâché masks, decrying some specific or vague aspect of human nature that is currently causing them particular sorrow.

I remember the 1970s in Plainfield, Vermont. I came back, two years after my graduation, to teach theater at Goddard College. In those days, the lads from Norwich Military Academy, in Northfield, twenty miles away, came over to Goddard to chase the girls. Those poor boys went to Vietnam. I and my friends did not. Now, in my mid-fifties I see the Fourth of July parade, and must vote with the veterans rather than with the Bread and Puppet Theatre. I do not think this is a sense of patriotism—I believe both groups are patriotic—but of proportion. Perhaps I am merely laying claim to a sense of belonging (even though vicarious) to that to which I do not belong. I find the Bread and Puppet Theatre smug and its cultural position a sinecure.

My farmhouse is at the site of the old town of South Woodbury. It stands crosswise to the road, and was once at the intersection of the South Woodbury Road. There are various fallen-in cellar holes nearby that mark the site of the town. South Woodbury moved some five miles away, down the hill, to the west, in the late nineteenth century. The graveyard remains.

Here we see graves with the small iron GAR marker.

Grand Army of the Republic, that is, the national forces in the Civil War. The American Legion sets small flags in the markers on Memorial Day. Here we find the graves of two Bailey brothers, who died in 1863, on the same day, in the same battle. In *Our Town,* Thornton Wilder writes of the New England Civil War veterans, "The United States of America. All they knew of it was the name. And they went and died about it."

I don't know. As I write, the administration seems to be raping the country; smiling, smirking, and emptying the coffers of gold. It insists on a so-called "tax relief" package that is a give-back to its paymasters. The Vermonters would see it as a species of the deplored "clear-cutting." In aphoristic form: You can shear a sheep many times, but you can only skin it once.

Perhaps one must submit to the ravages of politicians as to those of any other plague.

My friend Ilse Krutak is a knitter. She hangs out her shingle on Route Two, "Ilse Knits," and sells to the occasional motorist. My four children have grown up in her beautiful sweaters, hats, gloves, jumpsuits. She told me she was knitting sweaters for the families of the victims of September 11th at the request of some notable national relief agency. "Well you know," another woman said to her, "those sweaters are all going to be taken by the people at the agency." Ilse nodded her head as if in agreement to a commonplace, then added, "Well, maybe some of them will get through."

What is the meaning of the Great Stone Face? Washington pundits called Vermont President Cal Coolidge impassive. Yet the Vermont face is not impassive, but circumspect. We see this circumspection in the great humorists: Buster Keaton, Charlie Chaplin, John Cleese—they never send up the joke. They are still, and in their stillness we see something deeper than their mere "personality."

The Vermonters and the Scots practice economy of words. This is not a reluctance to communicate, but a desire to communicate only those things of which one is sure, and upon which one intends to act.

In the cities, words are used to charm, to seduce, to misdirect. Here we are expected to say what we mean; those who use words otherwise will be held accountable, perhaps considered fools.

Beloved craggy faces of my youth were those of the Vermont Transit bus drivers.

In the days before the interstate, they negotiated the run up from Boston on two-lane Route 14. I remember the coffee stop at White River Junction, where one frequented the Four Deuces Diner, or—if in extraordinary funds—the bar of the Hotel Coolidge, with its huge mural of something-or-other that I have forgotten.

I remember the impossibly narrow and acute switchbacks as the road passed beneath the railway trestles. Terrible weather, glare ice, sleet storms, perfect comfort in the buses. Who was driving? That fellow with the craggy face, and the badge on his shirt reading five, ten, twenty years without an accident.

As the road ran south, the country became gentle. As it does by Woodstock, Quechee, Brattleboro. I always thought of it as super-northern Massachusetts.

My Vermont is not gentle. It is beautiful and various and

changes valley to valley—old farm homes, fascinating to watch the way the builders accommodated the land, the exposure to the sun, protection from the winds and snow. Much of the charm of these houses lies in their rational situation, their active relationship with the geography. They have the human beauty of an act of understanding, the beauty of a tool. They are a testament to endeavor and a recognition of human limitation.

CHAPTER NINE

Some Personalities

The computer is a solution to no known problem. As such it must be seen as a Trojan horse, a false gift. A hammer, on the other hand, is a boon; as in a relationship with any friend, we smile, and love it for its very blemishes.

Is it accidental that the crafts flourish in Vermont?

They grow in an atmosphere of virtue.

Buggy Morse and Barbara ran the Lower Cabot Store.

He was a Cabot boy, and bore the local tradition of the town nickname. We have Nookie, Spud, Bozo, Bunchy, Dude, Moose, Chunk. Good names, all with good consonants, therefore names to call a dog with, or to shout out across a field, or a noisy shop, mill, quarry.

But I am romanticizing. I don't know where the names

came from. They seem to have begun in the Korean War generation.

Buggy always offered me a cup of coffee and a cigarette. I shot the breeze and traded guns with him. He had in his garage the actual American icon: the car the little old lady drove only on weekends to get the mail—a mint 1970 Caddie—up for sale in 1989 for $2,000. Fool that I was, I did not buy it. Why? Because it was too good to be true. The atrophy of the analytic sense in the face of potential good fortune. But, as Hazlitt says, "I did not enter that race."

That the deal was fantastical, and therefore disquieting, should have been offset by the identity of the dealer, who was a kind soul and an honorable man. (Stanley Baldwin described the Edwardian politician Sir Robert Horne as "that rare thing, a Scots cad.")

Deane Davis was governor of Vermont from 1969 to 1973. He was also a Superior Court judge and a lawyer, and a hell of a writer. His book *Justice in the Mountains* contains—and indeed addresses—the quintessence of Vermont humor. Business is business, he explains, and parties do business at arm's length, but there is, as part of the mountain ethos, a clear line between sharp practice and fraud. One may embellish and distract, but one may not lie.

A story from the governor's book: A man thinking himself bilked in a horse trade hauls the offending seller before a judge. "He sold me a horse with the heaves," the victim says. "And I asked him, straight out, and he said the horse didn't *have* the heaves."

"Is that true?" the judge asks the accused.

"No, Your Honor," he says. "He asked me, and I said, 'If this horse's got the heaves, *I've* got the heaves!' And, by god, Your Honor, I *have* got the heaves."

Reminds me of Albert May, "the Man who Wears the Derby Hat," and his auctions up at Molly's Pond: "This cup has a small nick in the rim. If you find that it does *not,* bring it back up here, 'n' we'll nick it."

In those days, the auctioneer was the local tribune, comic and pundit, interspersing his spiel with witty half-references to so-and-so's drinking habits, financial state, child-rearing capabilities, and treading damn near to who-was-sleeping-with-whom.

One evening Albert was holding down the auction stage, and there, out the open shed back, sitting in a tree, was some hippie chap, his overalls frayed into nothingness, and his essentially bare lower half exposed to the autumn winds.

Albert hardly broke stride. "Five, I've got five, do I hear five-fifty?..." Looked out the back, up at the hippie, and said, "... little late in the year, be seeing nuts in the trees ... Five-fifty, do I have *six?*"

The auctioneer would spiel, flanked by his spotters, who would call out the presence of the new bid.

"Six, and a *half?*... And a *half,* will you go the half?..."

"*Yuh!*"

"Six-a-half, now seven. Seven? Will you go it? Seven?..."

"Yuh."

"Now *eight,* will you go *eight?*... I got ya, Sally, hold on. Seven, seven, will you go *eight?*..."

And a man at the back would chop his flat palm across his chest, meaning "I'll go the half."

"Senn, a half ... Senn a half? *Sold!* To number?... Hold up your number, Chuck. Well, then, go *get* a number. Sold, next number! Bring it out, bring it out—what we got?" (Of some artifact his helpers now bring out.) "Well. That's some rig, there ... That's a nice one, that's about as fine a ... *anyone* know what this is? Gimme a dollar" (Hands shoot up.) *"All* over the house ... wall, then, gimme *half* a dollar. Sold! Bunchy Morton. Number?..."

Bunchy owned the town garage—now passed down to his son, Mike. I ran into Bunchy one predawn, out hunting. I'd been lying on the hill, waiting for false dawn, looking for the deer that would be rising from their beds to get down to the pond to drink.

I'd missed them, or more to the point they'd not missed me, so I got up and walked back toward the road, thinking to try the opposite field. And there was Bunchy in his pickup, dressed for hunting. He stopped and we chatted. He invited me to come down to Woodbury, to chuck all this early nonsense, and join him at the church in their hunter's breakfast. It sounded so good, I could taste the good acid coffee, but I demurred. I passed, I think, from a sense of foreignness.

I took a hunter's safety course. The course was taught by Larry Thompson. Those wishing a hunting license had to spend some eight hours studying the rules and safe handling of firearms. Good course. Good teacher. On the test I missed one question about the longest effective (that is, harmful) range of shotgun pellets. I am nothing whatever of a shotgunner, and had chosen 25 yards. Larry called me in for a post-exam consultation and corrected my estimate to 100 yards. I am sure I will never forget that range, though the content of the questions at which I succeeded has probably long fled.

Is there a lesson in this?

There is an old New England custom called bumping. The father walks the young son around the boundaries of the land. At each significant mark—a tree, a stone, a dead stump— the boy is brusquely pushed by his father, bruised against the marker.

As I age, wisdom increasingly seems to me just the absence of foolishness. Over the decades the number of situations in which one has bruised oneself accumulates. Those encounters sufficiently abashing, humiliating, sobering to leave a bruise are remembered, and avoidance of their repetition I will class— at least in my case—as wisdom.

A Vermont story: Bill Corrow was mowing my field, out by the pond. I came over to chat, and he said he'd planned to have his daughter come out the next day to finish up.

"I thought I'd ask, do you mind a woman doing the work?"

"No," I said, "why should I mind? I like women. I married one of 'em."

"Dave," he said, "you married *two* of 'em," and drove off on his tractor.

Another story, also treating of marriage:

I was in the midst of a divorce. As part of the settlement, my ex-wife listed several objects she'd like to take from the Vermont house. I was off somewhere making a film, and returned to Vermont, surprised to find that she had, impromptu, elaborated her list. Every last object in the house was gone. The window shades, the toilet-paper rollers, the match safe screwed into the wall—indeed, the very plants and bushes ringing the house. Everything was gone.

I sighed, hopped into my truck, and drove to Berlin, twenty miles away, where I knew there was a furniture store.

I walked in and nodded at the salesman.

"I need some furniture," I said.

"You sure *do....*" he replied.

Having ventured as far afield as Berlin, I will drift down to East Barre, and the antique store of Ed Farr.

This is the real thing. Nelson Algren cautioned us never to play poker with a man named Doc, never to eat at a place called Mom's, and never to sleep with a woman whose problems are worse than our own. I will add to that list (you may find it in *The Man with the Golden Arm),* never buy an antique in a store selling anything that might remotely be classed as a reproduction, reiteration, homage, gift, or words to that effect.

Ed's store (now in Danville [see the American Society of

Dowsing]), the result of his continual and canny scouring of the Northeast, the stuff out back of the barn. It contained treasures.

I was shirking work one day, and pulled up at his store to chat. And there was a Civil War, walnut rolltop desk. The pulls were hand-carved bowers of walnuts, the rolltop worked perfectly. It was, for a writer who "lives in Vermont," *the* accoutrement.

Now, I have (as, perhaps, have you) tended to shun the aphorisms of self-indulgence: "Buy a good watch. A man doesn't *have* jewelry, just the one piece, so you *should* indulge yourself." "Get the options on your car, you spend one-umpteenth of your life in the car." Et cetera.

I have always distrusted these easy dispensations of luxury. And then I have embraced them (as, perhaps, have you).

So there I was, a writer who had no "tools of the trade," save those that could be purchased at the dime store for 89 cents. And there was the world's most perfect desk, price $2,500.

This was in the early '80s, and quite a lot of money; too high a price for me. So, of course, I went outside, took a deep breath, came back in, and gave him a check.

That night anxiety struck. How, I wondered, could I so indulge myself? Was it not vile luxury? What might the notional forces governing Inspiration think, were I to beard them by suggesting I required anything other than a table on which to rest my notebook?

I called Ed Farr, and sheepishly explained to him that I thanked him, and wished him no inconvenience, but I would appreciate it if he'd simply tear up the check.

"I will not," he said, "I'm going to deliver the desk tomorrow, and for years to come *you're* going to thank me."

He did, and I do.

I know of a man who, I was told, never bought anything that he could not subsequently sell for a profit. For a while I envied that man his perspicacity, incisiveness, and mercantile sense. Then it occurred to me that I am not a merchant, and he could go with God. "I did not enter that race." The desk, I presume, has appreciated substantially—but that, of course, was not Ed's meaning.

I recall the Wooton desks displayed for sale at the New York Armory show. These Edwardian contraptions (favored, I think, by Teddy Roosevelt) present as a four-foot-high cylinder, or "miter"; the two doors swing open, and swing open again, to reveal a maze of drawers, cubbyholes, recesses, secret panels. Beautiful. Year by year I'd see the prices: $2,000; next year, $8,000; next year, $17,000. And each year I'd think, *"Outrageous!"* and, "If only I'd bought it *last* year...."

But my distracted or pathetic (choose one) nonmercantile soul bought the Vermont place for a song (fifty grand for the house and one hundred acres), and I've treasured every moment I've spent there.

I take that back. Once I got lost in the winter woods. I was inappropriately dressed, I didn't have a compass, I got turned around, bone-cold and wet, hungry, and the sun went down. My body temperature dropped, and I got hypothermic.

One of the symptoms of hypothermia is dementia. One

begins to lose one's mind and behave insanely. People have been known to strip naked in the snow, to climb trees in a thunderstorm. There are cases of a lost traveler's tracks being seen to stumble onto a traveled road and then back again into the woods, where they led to the corpse.

I, too, have known such missteps. One day I was walking what I took to be the bounds of my land. I trod into what I found was a blowdown. Up to my armpits, I had to struggle to pull myself out. I emerged sweating, chilled, and panicked. The sun went down. And I began to run toward what I hoped was the road.

Several hours later, having crossed my own tracks at least twice, incapable of remembering either the goal or the purpose of my frenzied flight, I stumbled out into a road, grateful and thrilled. I was half a mile from my house.

Aside from that, I've had a pretty great time.

I bought some adjoining land from Charlie McCarty. He was the real deal.

I was thirty something, and he was in his seventies, and he walked me over his land. He was puffing and huffing the whole way, and concluded a several-hour tromp through the blowdown puffing neither more nor less than when he had begun. I spent the bulk of the walk wishing for death, in preference to another fifty yards at his pace.

I remember fishing on West Hill Pond with Charlie. He said, "Let's catch some perch," and we caught perch for an hour. Then he changed lures and he said, "Let's catch some pickerel," and we caught pickerel. He was said to be descended from the Hatfields and/or the McCoys of Southern Animosity Fame.

I wish he was still with us. I regret that I never went hunting with him.

Charlie died and his friend George Twine inherited his firearms. I asked if they were for sale. And George said, "Sure." I bought a rather rundown Parker shotgun, 12-gauge. That is Parker, the finest American shotgun ever made. This version, circa 1915, was the lowest grade, no frills, no ejector, no engraving, low-level checkering; and it was beat-up (what the auctioneers call "honest use") into the bargain. But I bought it, and took it to the gunsmiths, and asked them if they could help—to what extent could they bring it back? They could make it look new-in-the-box, 1915, they said. And they did. (New England Gunsmiths, Lebanon, New Hampshire, by the way.)

Also at George's, out in the barn, I found the table.

My friend Greg, at that time, had a house about two miles from me, up West Hill Road. In the house he had an old country-store worktable. It was about 3 by 5½, butcher-block maple, on roughly turned spruce legs. The table was deeply scarred, as it had been used for butchering. Sanded down and oiled, it beamed in his kitchen. And here, in George's barn, was another of the same. It had a history: This table had come out of the East Montpelier store on Route Two, where as a lad I had bought cigarettes.

George was using it for a reloading bench. It was backed up to a wall, and covered with boxes of shells, tins of powders, boxes of bullets, reloading manuals, scales, and an impressive stratum of lead dust.

I asked George if it was for sale. He was noncommittal.

I started mentioning various prices, and he remained the same. I could not, it seemed, break him free.

At the poker game I asked Alan, a Vermonter born and bred, how to proceed. "Stop by, give him a check, and ask him to help put it in the truck," he said. I did.

Alan is a ringer. He says "Ayup" and "Nope" in the best Vermont tradition, and in that sweet, curt accent that is, unfortunately, disappearing.

I spent a vast amount of my youth with Alan, as we both played in the same poker game. Consider fifteen or more hours a week for twenty years. He looks and acts like the old farmer, which for a stint he may have been, as one of his many incarnations—including, I discovered after some years, state historian of Vermont.

In his seventies, he is, as of this writing, a ski bum.

Where was I? The table, cleaned up, in my kitchen, and I took a hunter's safety course.

One of my fellow students was Jack, a man of about my age. At the second course he greeted me, "Hi, Mike!" He smiled with that deserved self-satisfaction we reward ourselves for remembering the name of a chance acquaintance, and I was loath to deprive him of it.

I see him these days only on the Fourth of July. His traditional viewing spot is near mine. "Hi, Mike!" he says, and I say, "Hi, Jack!" and smile. I enjoy being called Mike.

I think everyone I ever met named Mike was a good fellow. Further, I think I have, if only in the restricted locus of my own fantasy, accepted it as my Cabot nickname.

Harry Thompson always remembers my name. I think he remembers everything. He must be in his mid-nineties, but looks to me just as he did in 1965. He is small, wiry, and has a gray and brown beard reaching considerably down the bib of his overalls.

He and his brother Dude dealt in antiques. One went to Dude and Harry's to find whatever it was one needed: a hand-cranked Victrola, an Argand lamp, a barn full of old shoes.

I remember Dude at the auctions. He, too, wore the bib overalls, the battered Gabby Hayes felt hat, and the beard. I recall him sitting in a rocking chair, a .38 revolver strapped in an aviator's holster across his chest, rocking back and forth.

Eliott Merrick left Yale in the 1920s and came north with his young wife to learn to farm. His 1934 book *Green Mountain Farm* treats of the area around Cabot and Craftsbury, where Merrick lived. I asked Harry once if he remembered the fellow. "Yes," he said. "Used to work for the school board."

The old story has a New York antiques dealer stopping by chance into Dude and Harry's. A run-down farmhouse, run-down barn, no sign, dead cars and junk in the yard.

The fellow comes in, looks around, sees nothing much, starts to leave. As he does so, he almost trips over the cat. The cat continues to its saucer to drink its milk. Fellow goes out in the yard and stops.

Was that, he thinks, what I thought it was?

He goes back in, and sure enough the cat is lapping milk from a priceless Ming Dynasty saucer, worth about forty grand.

"You know," says the fellow, "I think I'm going to buy that old tricycle after all. And, I suppose, these Chase and Sanborn coffee tins."

"Alright," says Harry. "That'd be, say, would you give two dollars for the tricycle?"

"Yes."

"Alright. Two dollars and, say, fifty cents for the two tins."

"And you know what?" the fellow says. "That saucer for sale?"

"Sure."

"I'll take that, too."

"Alright," Harry says. "Tricycle, coffee tins, and the saucer—that'll be thirty-eight thousand, two dollars, and fifty cents."

The story is, of course, too good to be true, and has additionally most likely been told as long as there's been an antiques trade. Nevertheless.

I see Harry now and then, at the Marshfield Village Store.

Each town had one. The store that was the market, fount of wisdom, post office, and seat of government. The tradition persists.

Nookie Thompson owned Harry's Hardware (the Cabot Country Store) when I arrived. Chris Kaldor came up with Ruth from Baltimore in 1980, and took it on. He's been the town clerk for the last twelve years. He and Ruth came up with nothing, and built a life for their family. Ruthie teaches art at the school, Chris built a house up across from Doc Caffin's place, above the town.

Looking at the houses arrayed on the hill, one sees Grandma Moses. Look across the valley and the houses are arrayed in one dimension, up and down. It is a primitive painting, or a quilt. A New England vision.

Chris and I try to get out in deer season to (as Alan says) "take our rifles for a walk." I remember walking up on Chris in the woods in a snowstorm. Chris is sitting on an old stone wall, rock still, so quiet, in effect, radiating calm and peace.

He has become such a Vermonter as to create and claim that sacrosanct badge of belonging, an inveterate feud. Throughout the years of his administration, he has been obstinately opposed by a town selectman, the axioms upon which his actions are based incapable of being rationally determined.

Chris, who could hold office 'til death if he desired, has now decided to retire. As the cop lays down the gun and the fireman the pike, Chris will have to renounce his patient execution of his sworn duties in the face of unfathomable perversity.

We, in the West, speak slightingly of "rug merchants."

The term is an indictment of what is seen as a non-Western (that is, a suspect, an unclean) way of doing business.

But in a market unmoored by published and (seemingly)

immutable prices, both the buyer and the seller must be assured that the final price is fair.

So the negotiation process of the souk—indeed, of the antiques store, the auction, the farmers' market—is, finally, a mutual interrogation: a dialectic intended to reveal the truth.

The Western concept of Scout's Honor is here rejected, supplanted by the no-fault understanding that each side will do business in its own best interest—and, therefore, that truth-in-utterance may neither be coerced nor enforced.

Here, in this "non-Western" dialogue, the parties, rather than endeavoring (in wisdom or folly) to set a fair price in concert, set out each on his own. And no stigma is attached to dissimulation.

For the rug merchant knows, as does the antiques dealer, that all business is lies, and that the cry "He's not playing fair!" is, in itself, the attempt to secure an unfair advantage.

The rug merchant is free with his oaths, discounting his own equally with those of his opponent; and is thus, perhaps, more humane in his dealings than are his Western counterparts.

For why should a price (any price) be other than negotiable?

The notion that bargaining is "just not done," that it is *déclassé,* un-American, indeed "Jewish," can operate only to the benefit of the seller—increasingly a conglomerate with the power of mass marketing, the potential for political and/or judicial subornation in its own defense, and a healthy and protected remove from the end user.

All commercial organizations have inducements to collude against the consumer. Most succumb to them, their horizontal community of interest overcoming any philosophic inclination toward competition or "fair trade."

For the law of supply and demand is, to the manufacturer, the circle that must be squared, a law in whose manipulation or contravention even the most neophyte merchant must perceive wealth.

The consumer agrees, in his turn, to accept the pleasant fiction of "an honest price," "the wisdom of the market," in denial of his common sense, his knowledge of both contemporary affairs and history.

The soothing myth is balm to his anxiety. It is, in psychic economy, a better bargain to accept the myth that "They (or someone) know what they're doing" than it is to tremble at each mercantile choice over the veracity of every claim of fairness, efficacy, or product safety.

The producer disappears behind the screen of conglomeration and remote, impenetrable administration. Management itself is further diluted into the vapor of stockholders and a board of directors, these parties not only unwilling but in fact incapable of ethical action when free—and, when apprehended, unable to cease shifting blame.

Advertising seduces the consumer into a fantasy, making it difficult to locate, let alone judge, any actual claims made for a product. (How, then, to judge the product's worth, and thus its legitimate price?) Any consumer capable of actually locating a verifiable claim, and finding said inexact, inflated, or fraudulent, will be hard-pressed to pierce the corporate defenses seeking redress (yes, perhaps, for a bar of soap, but what of the woman rendered infertile by an intrauterine device?); and those seeking redress in our society are liable to the epithet "crybabies"— that is, "incapable of looking out for themselves." A sympathetic response to such woes is not shock but "What did you expect?"—the umbrage of a society deadened by the everyday frauds we encounter in the name of "business."

This or that organization claims to "be our friend," to have listened to or anticipated our needs.

But in the dawn of disillusion, should we have been so dense not only to buy the product but to believe its claims, our friend is gone.

Enron executives had transcripts made of one of their councils of war when the news of their collusions began to break. "Someone" then had those transcripts shredded. Wailed Enron's top management: "But those transcripts would have *exonerated* us...."

How much better the self-respecting self-interest of the bazaar.

CHAPTER TEN

Empire and Village

Will Hamlin taught English at Goddard College when I was a kid.

He wrote the catalogue that, in the '60s, attracted the young to the school. ("Goddard's students are regarded as unique individuals who take charge of their own learning. Through collaboration with faculty and staff, Goddard encourages students to become creative, passionate, lifelong learners, working and living with an earnest concern for others and for the welfare of the Earth.") An interesting vision, *vide* Isadora Duncan in the Edwardian period, the nineteenth-century American Utopians, indeed, the Stoics, who taught that all that is required for a school is a teacher, a student, and a board for them to sit upon.

Goddard had the board, in the shape of the lovely, Victorian Martin Estate. Martin got rich, as I understand it, by inventing or manufacturing tank treads. He fleshed out the family farm with stone buildings and formal gardens; Goddard came along in the late '50s, bought it up, transformed the barn into offices and meeting rooms, the mansion into offices and housing—and, in a period of growth, threw up eight or so unforgivable siding-covered boxes and called it the Village for Learning.

The tenor of the school can be gleaned from the study of far better satirists than I. I suggest Mary McCarthy's *Groves of Academe,* Randall Jarrell's rival *Pictures from an Institution,* and much of Nabokov.

The board existed, and the teachers and the students might have been found, in colloidal form, in an ooze of license and self-delusion.

I had a good time there.

Thirty years later I was having dinner with Will. "You know, Will," I said, "looking back, there really wasn't a school there—just a catalogue."

"No," he said, "that's right."

I recall him, in the '60s, at some all-school meeting, as he spoke with passion about the destruction, nay desecration of Vermont.

His view was, of course, correct. The inevitable incursion of the cities—Burlington, Montpelier, Boston, Montreal—ensures the transformation of Vermont into Connecticut. Soon it will be gone, as Will saw it would be gone in 1960, as Eliott Merrick feared in 1930.

I am privileged to have lived there. Neither was I a neutral. My presence, my understanding of the area as picturesque and rare qualifies me as a despoiler—or, to put it differently, as a (legitimate or not) inevitable part of the cycle of growth and decay.

Vermont was deforested in the late 1800s; the timber of today was planted in the 1950s. By the 1920s, the native deer, deprived of their habitat, had gone.

Latterly the moose population has been growing. Wolves have been seen, come down from Canada, and the catamount (mountain lion) is back. I know it is, because I've seen it, just up the road from my house. Bear and turkey and deer doing well, so here we have a twist in the helix.

I will be gone, and some studious soul will note that a writer, in the late twentieth century, lived in a farmhouse in what is now a suburban subdivision—*could* there have been bear and lion there, such a short time ago?

Tom Paine warned us that faction is the enemy of good government. We view this statement wistfully, as today it is all of government we know.

We might opine, as did Marshall McLuhan, that the fact of an advertising campaign is important, but its content is not. And must not every dollar spent on advertising represent one dollar of obligation the politician owes to some master other than the voter?

One looks at the matter-of-fact subornation of officials in Washington, and wonders: Is the geometric increase in rascality between the village and the empire simply a matter of the square of the distance from the afflicted to the official?

Must not the political corporation, like the commercial, grow until, unable to support its elaboration, it falls of its own weight?

And what of our beloved justice? Once, in the village, we knew the folks but not the crime. Now, increasingly, the crime is not a mystery, but we, as the jury, know nothing of the accused. How may we judge them?

The illusion of impartiality means, to a large extent, the excision of reason. The possibility of impartiality being seen as a sham, it was considered reasonable to replace it with randomness, and deem it respectable to manipulate a random throw of the dice through bribery and manipulation. Gibbon wrote that the decay of the empire was hastened by the proliferation of lawyers; and that, were it not bad enough that they (for a price) argued that black was white and all was relative, they after a time inevitably came to believe it.

Well, these same debauched lawyers provide the applicant pool from which come our candidates for office—folks who have been taught that it is reasonable to set aside compassion, common sense, and community feeling in the service of that higher good: justice.

It is said that a liberal is a conservative who's been arrested. I add that a conservative is a liberal who's been mugged. I, a congenital liberal, increasingly feel mugged by my government. What am I to do, and is my dilemma a predictable adjunct of growth? I live at the crux of the American hegemony, sufficiently close to the summit to see—indeed, to feel the pull of—both slopes.

The road to my house has not changed in two hundred years. The houses were built of hewn first-growth pine. And in one hundred years—in fifty years, perhaps—the dirt road will be paved, the paved road will be lined with homes, the bear, wolf, fox, moose, mountain lion will be gone, as the woods will be gone.

I am not bitter. Why should I be? I am as much a cause of the change as anyone else now alive, who, in our agglomerate, need someplace to live, and who are entitled to live.

Some must select themselves to be my beloved recluse artisans, and subsistence farmers. Perhaps I feel that my admiration of them decreases or shades my own shameful consumerism. Some must select themselves to go to Washington, and live off the fat of the land and the distance from a confused electorate. Yet in Vermont we have the House of Representatives' only socialist, Bernie Sanders, and the celebrated Senator Jim Jeffords. Jim crossed the aisle, deserting his Republican Party and its ways. He bunks with the Independents, but effectively weighs in with the Democrats, and broke the back of the Bush Senate by his change.

Jeffords was hailed for his heroism. I think his act should also be noted for its rarity: If our officials are not to follow their conscience and common sense, what, in effect, *are* they to do?

And the answer is, they will take their legal training, continually confuse ends and means to the debauchment of both, and (in a final decay into intellectual savagery) come to believe that there is, in their tergiversations, some service of some greater good: that, in the fool phrase of the '60s, "the system works."

Does the system work? It must. Containing, as it does, such mindlessness. It must work in the service not of some greater good, but of an unknowable progression of decay. I cite the innumerable science fiction novels of my youth, in which it is discovered that the world is but an atom, neutron, electron, and that its explosion (from nuclear war, to name a favorite) is but one of some untold trillion atomic events—which, in their entirety, constitute but one infinitesimal gamma ray (or some such) in the macro world. How could an intelligence in that world, wonders my adolescent mind, conceive, let alone understand, the worries of some confused Jewish kid on the South Side.

Well, the big wheel runs by faith, and the little wheel runs by the grace of God. The politician throws his or her suit coat over the shoulder and nods in understanding at the crippled child, and we've still got to go down to the store for a quart of milk.

First Tuesday in March, Vermont law says there is to be a town meeting, at which the voters will approve or disapprove the budget and various other ordinances. They shall do so by a *show of hands.*

This year there is a heated debate, as some faction in town is plumping for the introduction of the Australian ballot.

My friend Chris, the town clerk, beaten into realism through his many years in office, shakes his head at the self-defeating headstrongness of humankind. I translate his gesture to mean: Can they not see that the voter *must* stand up and declare himself—that the possibility of creating enmity in his neighbors by an unpopular vote is a necessary mechanical and *positive* component of the open vote? The town government works only when (and because) people are willing to put their names on what they believe in.

Better the enmity of the small town than the confected antagonisms of the hypocrites in Washington, familiars of big business.

Alan Soule invariably refers to "lawyers" as "liars."

If the government has no ability to defend against the real threat of terrorists, but untold wealth to squander in the name of a "rogue missile launch," then the organism is in irreversible decay. The fantasy wish for an opponent who would, by his military actions, *endorse* our military-industrial complex by the nature of his aggression suggests a country that no longer wishes to survive.

But this is, essentially, the error of all bloated plutocracy— indeed, of King Midas, who strove to turn all life into gold.

Last year Bush et al. wiped out a vast budgetary surplus. This year, there is not enough money to rebuild New York. Tolstoy said that no intelligent man, looking around, ever said other than that the depravity of the world was so great that, surely, it must soon end.

The United States abrogates common sense, humane treaties on global warming, land mines, ballistic missiles, for the supposed benefit of a few businesses. One wishes to cry, "Shame!"

I think of the Great Wall of China, the Maginot Line, *Festung Europa*—all useless defenses displaying wealth and in fact inviting invasion. They are an attempt to defend not against a real enemy but against time and entropy, which can be placated only through self-abnegation and humility *(vide* the post-and-beam house).

The tree cannot survive the winter by putting out more leaves. The more a waning civilization tries to preserve the status quo, the more it vitiates those resources that might have supported it through a period of famine.

The institution must see any diminution—of power, of scope, of treasury—as anathema; this horror of change, time and again, is a spur of its very acceleration.

The Scottish framers knew that the heavy oak door warps, the light pine panel door expands, contracts, and survives.

I had a fear as a child. I had read that successful Japanese businessmen traditionally gave away all they had at age fifty, and took up life as wandering mendicants.

Why this frightened me I cannot say, as I am not Japanese, and stood not the remotest chance of becoming successful.

Perhaps it had to do with my fear of losing my father.

He had been very poor, had made some money as a lawyer, and at one point lost some or all of it in the stock market. We were never other than comfortably middle class, but it did not take much to awake in him the fear of poverty, and for him to share it with his family.

Here in Vermont I am not that different (if different at all) from those folks in the plaid pants, or from the leaf peepers. I make my living in another world, and take that largess, that urbanity, that lack of community, perhaps, to a cleaner land and, in coming, despoil it.

There are wheels within wheels. My coming to Vermont is part of the same tropism that leads potentially rational men and women to insist on increases in the defense budget. This book is likely to survive when the Corduroy Road (aka County Route 2) is gone.

Oh, if I had only been in on the desecration, one says, of the American West, of Connecticut in the '30s, of Cape Cod in the '50s....

In our dream of a pristine world, of a perfect environment, of the Garden of Eden, we inject ourselves, in fantasy, to despoil.

For we cannot resist the tree of knowledge. It is the tree of life and it is the tree of death, and having eaten from it we are doomed to both.

CHAPTER ELEVEN

The Village Restaurant

Greensboro Bend is a wealthy Yankee summer community: North Shore, Main Line, Westchester folks, pressed shirts and slacks and skirts—indeed, the occasional white belt.

Greensboro is on Caspian Lake. Good swimming, boating, fishing; the Highland Lodge up the hill, the many cottages and homes "dotted," as they must be, all around the shore.

It's ten minutes or so down the hill from Greensboro to Hardwick.

I love Hardwick. I eat breakfast every day at the Village Restaurant (junction of Routes 14 and 15).

The Village is open, I think, every day of the year, at 6 A.M. (during hunting season, hunter's breakfast at 4).

When Mary Mericier owned the place, the policy was that men got their coffee in a mug, women got theirs in a cup and saucer. Home-baked bread and pastries, eighteen-wheelers gearing down outside for the traffic light, the same regulars every day.

The folks who come down from Greensboro, though, cannot relax.

I watch the lines in airports. The well-to-do *perform* waiting in line. The rest just wait in line.

The Greensboro folks in Hardwick, similarly, perform a very good rendition of the brotherhood-of-man meets (let us not avoid it) fiscal and social—we need not say "inequality," but *difference.*

"Yes," their grin and posture proclaim, "we understand, we are not Vermonters. Although we have been coming to the area for *x* generations, we do not consider ourselves Vermonters. You, of Hardwick, are the true Vermonters.

"And we would never judge you—how *could* we, as we are of the same worth? Please pardon us as we, in what is essentially *your* restaurant, eat our eggs." Well, I am also a ringer. And I am also cursed with self-consciousness. But not, I hope, at the Village Restaurant.

They have home-roasted turkey with gravy over home-baked bread, iced tea and chopped chef's salad in the summer, and a view of the Lamoille River, out the back.

The Village leans out on supports over the river. In the drought summer of 1996, there was a three-day wonder: Some top-shelf and rare loon landed in the river out back. The water was already low, and fell sufficiently during the night that the bird lacked the runway needed to take off.

And the Fish and Wildlife wardens and curious others came to look on and marvel. I would tell you the end of

the story if I knew it. Those interested might apply to *The Hardwick Gazette,* which is the next building down Main Street from the Village Restaurant.

Continuing down the street we have Tom and Mike Brochu's service station. The twins are the best mechanics I've ever found, truly decent fellows, and I'm grateful to Mike for growing a mustache to aid identification. Across the street is the Buffalo Mountain Co-op, where we buy our food. The co-op movement is one of the blessings the hippie generation brought to Vermont. It is good for the consumer, and it supports the local organic farmer. It has several brands of local, artisan-baked bread, farm-made cheese, and vegetables including the elusive fiddlehead fern.

Angus from the co-op will not patronize the Brochus'; the garage has, in the window, a TAKE BACK VERMONT sign.

This indicates the sign-posters' opposition to Vermont civil union.

The law was passed in 2001, permitting couples unable (or, indeed, unwilling) to avail themselves of state-licensed marriage the legal protections of that benefice.

Curiously, it always seemed to me that Vermont had a rather high number of visible, long- and short-term homosexual relationships. I do not include my hippie generation and its various performances of experiment and license, but of the actual old-style Vermont village life. There was and is the Vermont tradition of folks leaving one another alone. The old saw has it that settlers coming north up the Connecticut River turned right to get to New Hampshire; to get to Vermont, they turned left.

But they always said that Oklahomans would vote their state dry as long as they could stagger to the polls.

Down around the corner is Linda Ramsdell's Galaxy Bookshop. She has kept an honest-to-God bookshop running in Hardwick for 14 years. And, I suppose, she is supported, in some notable part, by custom from the Greensboro summer people, so perhaps I should shut up.

Across the bridge, back in the '80s, across from the library, and next to the police station, was the gun factory. One half of the building was the X Natural Foods store. The other half was Caspian Arms. Cal Foster and his family and crew made highest-quality parts for the 1911 pistol (known generally as the Colt .45 automatic). Cal sold these parts to the top-of-the-line manufacturers of the piece; later he sold them the entire pistol, and still later he sold variations under his own brand. The food store sold, in the main, bulk products. The store is gone and Caspian moved out Route Fifteen to Wolcott. Too bad. Visiting the two made an interesting morning.

I bought a Civil War safe in Hardwick, Vermont. I bought it from Dave Maunsell, whom I knew from the Village Restaurant.

It is about three by two by three. It rests on casters. The casters are set perpendicular to the front of the safe.

Dave explained that this was to prevent the safe being wheeled out of the shop by villains. The safe would be installed, and bookcases, shelves, you-name-it would bracket it in, and there it was 'til doomsday.

Doomsday, in this case, being my purchase of the beauty. Dave and his son manhandled the monster up a ramp, into their truck, and waved off my offer of help. They drove it the seven miles to my house, and manhandled it down the ramp and into place in the cabin. I asked what I owed them for the move, and they refused to accept my money. I explained that I could not take their effort and time for free, and Dave said he had *understood* that delivery was to be part of the price ($175).

The safe sits next to the rolltop desk. It has, as I remember, some old coins in it, and a .22 Ruger "SingleSix" revolver I bought (new-in-the-box) for my son, eight or ten years before he was conceived.

Shooting had, 'til recently, been an important part of life in Vermont for me. I learned marksmanship in the Boy Scouts. That is, I learned about firearm safety, cleaning, and how to obtain a sight picture, squeeze the trigger, and there you have it.

In my late thirties I decided to get serious. I did so because I was bored. I sat all day in my cabin in the woods and, believe it or not, at some point(s) in those six to eight hours a day times three-hundred-plus days a year, inspiration waned.

I found I could both clear the head and pass the time through marksmanship. So I set up some targets out back of the cabin, and started to shoot. After some months of several hundred rounds a day, I began to hit what I was aiming at.

My standard, for myself and for the gun, was the ability to hit a nickel at 25 yards.

One thing led to another, and my interest in marksmanship metastasized into an interest in gun trading.

In those days (but still, perhaps, today) most small towns had a sporting-goods store, a gun store, or a general store or even a gas station where one traded guns. This certainly got one out of the house of a morning. It provided a destination, an excuse, a lot of very good conversation, and some useful information on shooting.

I began to compete with the pistol, both in bull's-eye shooting and in combat-style events sponsored by the International Practical Shooting Confederation.

It was, to a city boy of a sejant profession, a real satisfaction to have the range officer say, "Nice shooting."

I liked pistol shooting because it developed skill. Its variables are, famously, only two: front sight, squeeze the trigger; and, as the minutest differentiation from right practice entails the grossest avoidance of the target, the opportunity for philosophical rumination is great.

But I got old, and the notion of actually having to clean the piece after I'd shot it seemed an unwonted intrusion on whatever may be my remaining time.

Also, my eyesight worsened. I remember my longtime neighbor Howard Fitzpatrick shooting with me. He was a

twenty-five-year veteran of the NYPD. He'd moved, as a retiree, to Vermont, and had become an investigator for the state. On retirement from that position, he became a private eye. He recently retired again, and he and Betty moved to New Jersey. The worst word in the English language, he told me, was "retired."

Howard told me that, in the Marines, he'd been on a troopship off Japan, waiting for the invasion, when the atom bomb was dropped.

"You must have been pretty pleased," I said.

"No, but my mother was," he said.

He told me that old cops, on the range, look like pecking turkeys. They've got the gun out and they're leaning forward, leaning back, trying to find that lost focal range.

I recall one spring, there had been a lot of break-ins in my area.

"Tell you what," Howard said. "You pack up as if you and your family are going to leave. We sneak back, we'll sit in the dark and *catch* 'em."

I regret not having done so.

CHAPTER TWELVE

Justice

My oldest daughter was six months old. It was New Year's Day, and ten or so below zero. I somehow conceived the notion that we needed air. So I bundled the two of us, and put her in the Snuggli, and walked the mile and a half down the hill. A beautiful, stone-quiet day. Down to the Millrace, the water frozen over the dam, one white trickle coming over the ice, you get the picture.

Up the hill, and it was cold cold cold. I got to Howard's house and gave up. Willa was awfully quiet, and I'm glad I stopped. We warmed her by the woodstove. Howard gave me some scotch, and some of Betty's homemade shortbread, and drove me and the now-warmed critter up the hill.

It did get colder in those days.

Another transplant to Vermont was Bob Krutak.

Bob and his brother-in-law, Eric Scholz, reconditioned my farmhouse. They built the addition, the cabin, and the barn.

Bob taught himself carpentry when he came over after the war.

He'd been a Luftwaffe glider commando. After the war he was a policeman in Bremerhaven, then a butcher and cook for the American forces.

He met an officer from Cabot, who offered to sponsor Bob and his family in the United States.

They packed up and arrived to find the officer gone. So there they were, in Cabot, Vermont, with no funds, no English, no friends, no job.

I remember him and Eric working, at forty-below, down in the open cellar of my house.

I remember talking with Bob one morning out on the porch. I was standing one step down from him, and he affectionately put his hand on my neck; a moment later I found he'd unthinkingly lifted me, with the one hand, up to his level.

I remember him and his wife, Ilse, at dinner, at my house, with Andy and Anita, Holocaust survivors.

He died three years ago.

Another notable area transplant is William Rehnquist.

Chief Justice Rehnquist is a homeowner in Greensboro, right up the hill from the Highland Lodge.

He purchased his house in 1974. The contract for the house, it has been noted, contained a "restrictive clause." This clause bound the purchaser—in this case, Mr. Rehnquist—to refuse to sell the house to "persons of Hebrew extraction."

Mr. Rehnquist claimed he never read the contract he signed.

Now, an ordinary layperson who purchased a home without reading the contract might legitimately be accused of folly.

But consider Mr. Rehnquist: Not only was he a lawyer, he was an actual jurist.

For such, well-apprised of the perils of signing a conveyance one had not read, his act must be understood as a deep testament of faith in his fellow man.

He entered my consciousness again for his role in the late election. There, as Chief Justice, he intervened to abrogate the laws of Florida, of the United States, and his own oft-stated personal and party convictions of the sanctity of states' rights, thus coupling (see above) human faith to whimsy. Was there ever such a man?

The desserts at the Highland Lodge are superb.

Patrick O'Brian writes, "When has a village reputation ever been wrong?" The rabbis, when asked "If we were to obey only one rule, which would it be?" said, "Don't lie." For if one cannot lie, one is unlikely to do that about which one would lie.

Perhaps this accounts for the openness in the village faces. There is enmity and strife in village life, but, I think, little hypocrisy.

The dirt road runs up to Hugo's place at the height of land.

I have now walked twenty years' worth of children to sleep the half mile up that road and back. I've skied up and down that road. Half a mile up the road, off-lead. My wife and I trained the dog on it. We practiced hand signals at fifty yards. Down. Stay. Come. She'd heel up to Hugo's place, and then

down the North Road to the field. Sit-stay, hold hold, and then we'd let her run: *"Off* you go...."

I'd ski with her, back in the woods, breaking trail in the deep snow, back to Jug Brook; the snow over her chest, and she'd bound and bound, grinning. She'd grin when we went looking for grouse. She'd naturally quarter the field—twenty yards out, right, across left, and back, and give me that look of well-bred patience all know who've ever hunted behind a dog: I'll go there if you *wish,* but there are no birds there.

Molly the dog.

After the height of land, the land flattens a bit 'til the quarry.

We'd discovered this place in the mid-'60s, an abandoned granite quarry, a mile back in the woods, off the Cabot-Woodbury road.

Forest on three sides, the fourth a rock face 150 feet high.

The basin was deep, filled with ice-cold stream water. Great swimming, and the custom was one had to swim nude.

Thirty years later I went back, to find not only the uninitiated to the cult of nature but, predictably, gawkers and, shame of the world, a National Park Service ranger. Or perhaps he was merely a Statie. In any case he had a Smokey hat, and was policing the conduct of the quarryites.

Lately, it seems, they've taken up quarrying again. I hear the explosions, now and then, from my house.

F-16s from Burlington—the Air National Guard, "the Green Mountain Boys"—used to practice low-level (*very* low-level) turns over my house. That was diverting, too. Once, the house started to shake and rumble, and I wrote that off to the subway, 'til I remembered the subway was four hundred miles to the south, and realized I was living through an earthquake.

It's otherwise pretty quiet.

The corporation must be a model of the mind.

As all organic activities must mirror the workings of the mind, but with this difference: The corporation cannot will its own diminution or dissolution. Each aspect of the corporation strives to take root and fight its battles within the organization as a whole; now claiming the organization's stated purpose as justification, and now, when inconvenient, opposing or subverting it. The stated goal—for the organization as a whole, as for each of its component members—is as irrelevant as the concept of "life" is as a conscious, governing principle. The goal is life.

Perhaps, then, it is foolish to tax the deviant with hypocrisy, or perhaps even with arrogance. All life is arrogant, which is why we delight in praising passivity—"American peace-lovingness," for example, or "non-macho behavior."

Such harmless praise is all the attention the concept will receive.

IBM, up in Burlington, suggested that its workers did not need to unionize. The company, it said, would reward loyalty with loyalty. The company created its own pension fund, to which the workers contributed, until in 2000 those wishing to cash out were informed that their money was gone.

This is perhaps a crime and certainly a sin, but is it hypocrisy?

Perhaps civility is more important than law. At least it inculcates, in its practitioners, some pride.

The cougar hunts from cover in the tree. Is this hypocrisy?

Why, like Aesop, take lessons from the animals? Because in them we see the operative principles of life, shorn of attractive, potentially self-delusive explanations. And if the animals can feel, can predict a hard winter, a drought, an earthquake, so then, perhaps, can we. Why should we be debarred?

Another argument for dowsing.

CHAPTER THIRTEEN

Occupation Marks

In *Poor White,* Sherwood Anderson wrote of a master harness-maker reaching out to his son: "A man who has a trade is a man," he says, "and he can tell the rest of the world to go to hell."

This fellow is overtaken by mass production, and then the automobile renders his very trade irrelevant.

But not the potters, the carpenters, the blacksmiths, not the weavers.

Kate Smith is a master weaver. She was taught by Norman Kennedy, who came over with Tommy Makem to sing, and stayed on to found the Marshfield School of Weaving, in Plainfield, Vermont.

I was invited by Norman to a waulking of the cloth. The woven tweed bolt is sewed back onto itself, making a circle of cloth perhaps fifteen yards long. The cloth is soaked in the creek, then, waterlogged, taken up to be waulked. The weavers and friends, I among them, sit around all sides of a long table. Each takes the cloth, twists it, thumps it down on the table, and passes it on. The water is driven from the cloth, the cloth shrinks to size, the waulkers drink and sing. There are traditional "waulking" songs through which one keeps the rhythm.

Well, this feels like being very close to the center of things.

Watching Kate prepare one of her old wooden handlooms feels that way, too.

It feels holy without feeling churchy—necessary human endeavor with no room for sin.

I have a sport coat made of Kate's tweed, and several blankets. I have a shawl in traditional homemade blue dye. It smelled odd for many years, as Kate set the color in a traditional way, using urine. It was, she told us, her husband's. The husband is gone; the shawl, twenty years later, is finally clear of his memory. Kate is still weaving. In her quality as Eaton Textiles she does historically precise reproductions, and repair, for museums. My wife and I spent an evening with her. Norman came by, and he sang and taught us "Brennan on the Moore" and "Jock O'Hazeldean."

Visiting is a big thing in my community in Vermont. The life is *very* social, and we tend to find ourselves at one another's houses several nights a week. Well, we have been together, many of us, for forty years. We have lived through various marriages, divorces, deaths, births, inspired abortive business ventures, and, more to the point, we just get a kick out of each other. New Year's Day at Anita's, Thanksgiving at Roy's house.

Our community, in the main, is Jewish.

Q: Are we Jews clannish?

A: Yes.

The term, of course, carries more than a whiff of opprobrium. It is, perhaps, even racially derogatory—first, generalizing a behavior from the practice of some members of a group, and then pejoratizing it. But, yes, we are clannish. Perhaps some Jews are not clannish, but then I wouldn't know them, would I?

My friends include Howard and Jane, writers; Anita, as mentioned before, who got out of Poland in September 1939; Andy, her cousin and my longtime poker companion, a writer and worker with the blind; Rick and Rhea, Rhea is a writer and Rick works for the State Office of Prisoners' Rights; Charlotte the potter; Steve Bronstein the blacksmith and his wife, Sandy, an attorney; Jules and Helen, the bakers; the Belenkeys, manufacturers of children's clothes (zutanos).

We visit one another, and meet, in the meantime, at Rainbow Sweets in Marshfield.

Rainbow's was founded by Bill and Trish and Connie twenty-six years ago. It sits on Route 2 and offers homemade and elaborate pastries, and café food. Friday and Saturday night are pizza nights. Bill and Trish (Connie left to become a private investigator) put their girls through college (Oberlin and Macalester) selling pastries on Route 2.

Newborn kids on the way home from the hospital, traditionally, are taken to Rainbow's to be shown around and weighed on the pastry scale. (Three of my four kids were.)

Sunday mornings there are cherry cheese Danish pastries, and it is a good idea to call ahead for them the night before.

What a joy. Come in for coffee: "Howard been in?... Rick

been in?..." And so and so, traveling, will call on Friday night from L.A., Paris, Cincinnati, just to make an appearance.

A lot of writers come to Rainbow's. Louise Gluck used to live nearby, and copies of two of her poems hang on the walls. Grace Paley has been known to come in, Howard Norman and Jane Shore, Joyce Johnston, and I, as above, are more than regulars.

Pizza night, a couple of years ago, I looked around and, moved to speech, said, "I love our Jewish community," to which several responded, "What Jewish community?" But as they say, "Two Jews, three opinions."

Jewish or not, it is a wonderful community to have been a part of. For the week after my daughter's birth, a basket appeared at our door each night at dinnertime. It held dinner for two and a bottle of wine. We have been living out of each other's kitchens for decades now—one of the great gifts of Vermont.

Steve and Sandy Bronstein live out back and down the road from Rainbow's. Steve let me come to his blacksmith's shop to make a knife.

How hypnotic the forge is. It is humming, and orange and hot, and the whole ambience is somehow welcoming—not welcoming, but *embracing*.

The fire is dangerous, the air hammer, the band saw are dangerous, hammering on the anvil in tandem is dangerous, but none of it feels dangerous. One must be and is conscious of safety, which feels like, and is, respect for the components of the process, but the process, like Steve, seems warm and instructive. "If you pay attention," the steel seems to say, "you will *see* how to shape the material." And, indeed, one does. As one does at Charlotte's studio.

I played poker at Andy and Charlotte's house for those many years.

Andy and Charlotte split up, and Charlotte, released or emboldened, gave us her rendition of the all-night poker game, as heard from her bedroom upstairs: "'Click-click...' 'Fuck you.' 'Click-click.' 'Fuck *you.*'"

Charlotte, like Steve, like Kate, is an inspired, generous teacher. Over the years she has let me, my wife, and my kids come in, learn to throw and glaze. We've made pots and bowls, cups. I made an ashtray.

Charlotte is a world-class potter. Some years back she created a line of paper cups, plates, Chinese-food containers, in porcelain.

She made them for Bergdorf's and, in an unfortunate pre-emption or savagery on the part, as I understand it, of some Japanese consortium, was robbed, ousted, and deprived of the rights to that work.

She comes up with a new vision every few years. Latterly she has been working with native potters in Mexico, and travels back and forth there regularly. Her house in Plainfield looks down the valley on the most beautiful view I've ever seen. Some cell-phone company wants to pay her a competence to put up a relay station or some such on her land. They tell her they can make it look like a tree. "Click-click. Fuck you."

Charlotte's daughter Maya was a newborn when I started playing poker on the hill. Now she and her husband, Jimmy Kennedy, own and run River Run Café, down the hill in Plainfield. It is the other "local" of our Vermont neighborhood. Breakfast and lunch Wednesday through Sunday. The food is superb country fare, Southern-influenced by the Mississippian Jimmy, who brought catfish to Vermont. As of this writing he is traveling as a competitor in various bass-fishing tourneys.

The question one asks now and then of Rainbow Sweets and River Run is: Why not expand? Their supporters, patrons, admirers, and beneficiaries, wishing upon them decay. What fools these mortals be.

Used to be, and perhaps still is, one could buy Charlotte's Pottery at River Run—she made their plates and cups; the T-shirts were designed by the great Ed Koren of *New Yorker* fame, a member of the group. He lives down in Brookfield, some forty miles away.

Ed is a member—in fact the assistant chief now, I believe—of the Brookfield Volunteer Fire Department. When Rick was constable of Plainfield, Ed made him a sweatshirt depicting one of his fuzzy critters in a Smokey Bear hat, with the legend: "Constable, Plainfield, Vermont." I hinted, and kvetched, and eventually got one reading, *"Friend* of the Constable, Plainfield, Vermont."

For I have a sense, of course, of inauthenticity. I am not on the VFD, nor am I a constable. I am not a farmer, nor an artisan. I am a writer.

I have written about Vermont. Various magazine articles, a novel *(The Village),* a film *(State and Main),* but on balance I must feel that as good an argument could be made for my being a destroyer as for my being a preserver of Vermont. Indeed, a better argument.

This is of course mawkish, and this is a poor way to express gratitude. Let me put it differently: I am grateful to have lived there.

I am particularly grateful to my neighbor Vermonters. To these hardworking, generally hard-pressed people, it must

seem that I toil not, neither do I spin. And perhaps they are right. Nonetheless I've been the recipient not of regular but of unabated kindness, patience, and good humor from them.

A carpenter, working at my place, told me that previously he'd been tearing down some home in Montpelier. He was in the process of demolishing what he said was a particularly stupidly conceived improvement in a staircase. He took the crowbar to it, and found scribbled on the back of the lath: "A fool is paying me to do this job."

Often I've thought that is how the more legitimate folk (more legitimate than I) must feel about me, the interloper.

CHAPTER FOURTEEN

Self-Reliance

Self-respect seems to me a better philosophy for a healthy society than the most outward-directed charity, compassion, or even justice. There can't be the taint of self-congratulation in true self-respect, and one is not in danger of paternalism or patronizing, *vide* charity.

Edwin O'Connor wrote in *All in the Family*, "I know the wicked flourish and all that; what kills me is the really crummy grade of wicked who flourish around here."

That's how I feel, reading the daily papers.

Enron has just imploded. This Ponzi scheme bought influence right and left (seventy-three percent of the Senate took their money; vast hordes of officials in the executive or judiciary have recused themselves from the investigation, as they too were on the take). The CEO of Enron was paid more than 200 million dollars in the last three years. At the end he sold off his stock while advising his employees that the time had never been better to invest in the company.

As an employee incentive, the management gave out rocks. They were smooth-polished stones, engraved on one side with the company name and on the other, with choice words such as "Integrity," "Trust," "Dedication," "Loyalty." To outdo Dickens, they quite literally took their employees' life savings and in return gave them a stone.

But again, can a village reputation be wrong?

The Stoics, I believe, would nod in recognition of the Vermont ethic. They put it this way: Admire only those things with which you can reward yourself; abhor only those things you have it in your power to avoid.

Chris Kaldor was struggling in his first years at the hardware store. He had two small children. He built them a playground-sandbox out back of the store, near the river. His neighbor told him he'd mismeasured, that the sandbox encroached six inches over the property line. Chris tore the structure down.

Wendell Bird used to be a milkman. When I met him, he ran the Howard Bank in Montpelier. I'd made an error, a rather large error, in writing a check, and the error was being taken advantage of by the recipient, a commercial concern. I called the bank, explained the situation, and asked them to stop payment. They said they would.

They subsequently paid the check. I called Wendell and explained the situation to him. I had talked to an employee, I could not remember whom, and there was no record of my call. He said alright, his bank would make good the loss.

Acts of reserve, of self-respect, of circumspection have struck me over my decades in Vermont. If they have not improved me, they have certainly improved those better than I. John McCain spent five years under torture in a Vietnamese prison rather than accept what he considered a dishonorable repatriation. I know nothing about his politics other than that he is a Republican, a Guelph to my Ghibelline. Perhaps, however, in the labyrinthine disaster of national politics one might begin with the same consideration as in the election of town clerk: Let us have someone with self-respect.

I was living in a house in North Montpelier in the '60s. One day a vacuum salesman arrived. I told him I was not interested, that I was not a particularly conscientious housekeeper, and that, into the bargain, I had no money. He was determined, however, and plumped for the right to demonstrate his machine.

He ground soot into the rug and vacuumed it clean. He cleaned the Venetian blinds with a cunningly fashioned attachment, he did this and that and then, in what was obviously the *pièce de résistance,* asked for permission to vacuum my mattress. Okay, I said.

He did so, then opened the bag and emptied its contents onto a large sheet of paper.

Come with me, he said, and we went out onto the porch.

The human body, he said, has umpty-umptillion skin cells, and sheds them all at the rate of something or other.

He took the paper bearing the bag's contents, twisted it into a spill, set it on the step.

Those shed cells, he said, migrate down into the mattress. Now; see what my machine cleaned out.

He set fire to the paper. What does that smell like? he asked.

Oh, my gosh, I said. No. It smells ... it smells like roast chicken!

That, he said, is what is in your mattress, that is your shed cells—and that is what my machine will clean.

I saw him go with reluctance, wishing I had had the funds to buy a machine. I had been humiliated by the very contents of my bed, and this fellow had come to sell me the solution.

Thirty-five years later, I woke up in the middle of the night and realized he had crumbled a cube of chicken boullion into the bag before he began the demonstration. Good thinking.

Down the road apiece, at Goddard College, we had another

traveling salesman. He wrote to the school, advertising different wares, and asked the school to post his ad. He sold articles for the trousseau or hope chest: linens, flatware, kitchen sets. He was making his annual tour of the region's colleges and would, if invited, come to Goddard on such or such another night, at the populace's request. "Calling," in effect, "all brides."

And, on such and such an evening, there he was. The Radical Lesbian Dorm had responded, inviting him round.

There he was, in the college cafeteria, a fat, middle-aged man in a bad suit. Bald as you could wish, spreading out his pots and pans, and there they came: the self-deleted daughters of the middle class, to do battle with the arrogant, male, brain-dead, most probably heterosexual capitalist exploiter pig.

They came naked to the waist, their breasts further enhanced by paint, their faces smeared similarly, kissing and fondling one another, frottage, and you-name-it, to affront the bourgeois.

I saw their entrance and left in chagrin and pity for the poor traveling man. Some hours later, I passed back through the cafeteria as he was collecting the girls' filled-out order forms.

I doubt those girls have continued in their radicalism, and they have almost certainly outlived the partner of that moment, but I'll bet many of them still have those pots and pans.

CHAPTER FIFTEEN

Seasons

TAKE BACK VERMONT, the signs read. The signs are stirring. Stark black on white, sans serif. Good layout. I believe they stand for intolerance, for nostalgia, for protectiveness or concern, which specifies *the other* as the cause of anxiety.

The sign is rather disquieting. Bill, at Rainbow Sweets, displays a dead-on parody reading "TAKE BACK YOUR EMPTIES."

I understand "TAKE BACK VERMONT" to mean: "Your rejection of hypocrisy affronts me. I will tolerate your kind as long and only as long as I am not affronted."

Quite the opposite of "How are things on your hill?"

That ancient Vermont greeting still survives, perhaps not untainted by an appreciation of its picturesque antiquity.

The more current Vermont greeting is exchanged between passing motorists. My pickup is going east, yours west. As we approach, each driver lifts his or her index finger (of the hand

on the wheel) languidly, briefly, and lets it fall. The salute may be accompanied by a slight nod.

As with many other meaningful interchanges, over-thought renders it invalid.

In Vermont life runs by the seasons.

We have mud season. Blackfly season, tailgated by deerfly season; deer season, subdivided into doe-bow-rifle and black powder; leaf season, sugaring, and the various regularities of the farm and woods—I note the prized appearance of fiddlehead ferns.

Likewise, the life of my neighbors seems to be regulated. It progresses through school and the military; through courtship, marriage, adultery, and perhaps a second start, a notable calamity, or a folly of some stripe; then on to illness and death.

Life is, no doubt, similarly regulated elsewhere. But here, in Vermont, the course of the thing seems clearer, to my eyes, less demeaned by obfuscation, self-delusion, and deception.

We Americans delight in self-deception. We seem, in fact, to insist upon it, in our foreign policy, in our tax code, in our traffic laws, in education, in politics, time and again confusing an advertisement with a promise.

Is this preferable to French cynicism, or British resignation? I don't know, but it is our own and we are stuck with it.

A town very near mine was for many years a speed trap. I was (wrongfully, of course) nabbed one day—my only traffic ticket in thirty years, and I was miffed.

The arresting officer was a rather nice, kind-looking and very young woman.

It occurred to me that I was speaking to her as one human being to another, and had omitted the ritual "What seems to be the trouble, Officer?"—a phrase that means, in effect, "Please don't kill me."

American police may require obedience to the laws, but they certainly demand a ritual display of subservience, the final exhortation to which is, as above, fear of death.

How odd, in a group hired to enforce our traffic laws. What is going on? We have elected the police our national superego.

We, as a culture, suppress so much, deny so much, that there must needs be a mechanism to balance our suppression of the savage id by the craven ego. We call this "conscience," or "respect for the law"—the police, the local and national organs of

enforcement, are lauded, are mythologized constantly in films and television. We are, in fact, in the process of adopting law enforcement as our national mission: to enforce peace upon the world.

The message of the policeman's extortion of obeisance is that it is better to die by the side of the road than to live in a world without hypocrisy.

This is a lesson of agglomeration, where the populace is made up of strangers and each person must rough out a culture based upon the fairly useless, certainly exploitive tools of the mass media.

Perhaps a speed trap is better than a tourist trap, and the demand "Pay me your fine and keep moving" is healthier than "Please stop and buy a nice hand-dipped candle."

I got the best of the best of Vermont.

I got to see, over almost forty years, the natural unfolding both of the seasons and of the lives of my neighbors.

So much of my own life there seemed artificial—the growth marks of the kids cut into the door frame, the wooden animals I carved for their birthdays, the wood I cut and chopped, the burial plot I bought.

I bought the plot from Sprague Bailey, the man from whom I bought the house.

It's in the South Woodbury Cemetery. You can see it from my kitchen window.

My purchase seemed to me not only artificial but something of a pretension—the fantasy that my children, one day, would visit my grave with their children. "You know, your grandfather, my father, used to say ..."

For who was I, even in fantasy, to inflict my self-conscious pomposities on yet another generation—and that unborn?

But the planes crashed on September 11. I took and take these Boston flights regularly, and I thought how terrible it would be, in that afterlife we all imagine as death, not to rest in Vermont.

ABOUT THE AUTHOR

David Mamet was born in Chicago in 1947. He has taught at the Yale Drama School, New York University, and Goddard College in Plainfield, Vermont. His plays include *American Buffalo, Glengarry Glen Ross,* and *Speed-the-Plow;* among his screenplays are *The Untouchables, Wag the Dog, Heist,* and *State and Main.* The many accolades he has received include a Pulitzer Prize, two Obie Awards, and two New York Drama Critics Circle Awards. He lives with his wife and their children in Vermont.

This book is set in Garamond 3, designed by
Morris Fuller Benton and Thomas Maitland
Cleland in the 1930s, and Monotype Grotesque,
both released digitally by Adobe.

Printed by R. R. Donnelley and Sons on
Gladfelter 60-pound Thor Offset smooth
white antique paper.

Dust jacket printed by Miken Companies.
Color separation by Quad Graphics.

Three-piece case of Ecological Fiber pine side
panels with Sierra black book cloth as the spine
fabric. Stamped in Lustrofoil metallic silver.